D0938317

Primer
of
Psychotherapy

Primer
of
Psychotherapy

A *Developmental Perspective*

Gertrude Blanck, Ph.D.

JASON ARONSON INC.
Northvale, New Jersey
London

Production Editor: Elaine Lindenblatt

This book was set in 12 pt. Times Roman by Alpha Graphics of Pittsfield, NH, and printed and bound by Book-mart Press, Inc. of North Bergen, NJ.

Library of Congress Cataloging-in-Publication Data

Blanck, Gertrude.
    Primer of psychotherapy: a developmental perspective / Gertrude Blanck.
      p. cm.
    Includes index.
    ISBN 0-7657-0286-X
    1. Psychoanalysis. 2. Developmental psychology. I. Title.
    BF175.45 .B57 2000
    155—dc21   00-038983

Printed in the United States of America on acid-free paper. For information and catalog write to Jason Aronson Inc., 230 Livingston Street, Northvale, NJ 07647-1731. Or visit our website: http: // www.aronson.com.

To the memory of Rubin Blanck
whose ideas live on

A Poet's Definition of Object Constancy

Let me not to the marriage of true minds
Admit impediments. Love is not love
Which alters when it alteration finds,
Or bends with the remover to remove:
O, no! it is an ever fixed mark,
That looks on tempests and is never shaken;
It is the star to every wandering bark,
Whose worth's unknown although his height be taken.
Love's not Time's fool, though rosy lips and cheeks
Within his bending sickle's compass come;
Love alters not within his brief hours and weeks,
But bears it out even to the edge of doom.
If this be error and upon me prov'd,
I never writ, nor no man ever lov'd.

William Shakespeare
Sonnet 116

Contents

Introduction

Although this book is intended as an introduction to psychoanalytic developmental psychology, I found that I could not deprive the reader of the latest, and in some instances more sophisticated, theoretical thinking. Therefore, the elementary concepts that I set out to present are interspersed with new ideas, some of which have not yet been published. That makes this book of interest to the experienced therapist and analyst as well as the novice.

Psychoanalytic theory, especially during Freud's lifetime, was a unitary theory of human pathology. Theorists such as Jung, Adler, and Horney who did not agree with Freud left the fold to form their own schools of thought.

Matters are not so simple today. Theories continue to proliferate. But now many innovations that might have been rejected by Freud are covered under the umbrellas of The American Psychanalytic Association and The International Psycho-Analytical Association regardless of how closely they hew to, or how far they depart from, that which is called Freudian, or *classical,* or *mainstream* or, lately, *traditional.* At this point there are, in addition to classical theory, interpersonal, intersubjective, relational, perspectivist, social constructionist, and still counting.

Some of the new theories are designated as two-person psychologies to convey the idea that the psychologies of both patient and therapist are involved in the action. By that characterization, *mainstream* theory is said to be a one-person psychology, implying that the analyst or therapist is uninvolved. This sets up a straw man in the form of the much maligned analyst as blank screen. It obliges me to state the obvious: there cannot be a one-person psychology while there are two persons in the consultation room, for that would suggest the absurd conclusion that the analyst has no personal psychology. The real issue is not the head count, but the different perspective about the role of the analyst. The mainstream analyst, just as much as the so-called two-person analyst, participates in the action. It is the action per se that differs. The difference lies in the use of the countertransference.

Mainstream analysts not only listen, think, and interpret, but also feel with, identify with, empathize, and are affectively touched. In the present era, they are not at all the stereotypical blank screen, an unfeeling instrument remote from the patient's affect. The issue revolves around how analysts use their thoughts and affects. They examine their own feelings, think about what is being instilled in them and use it to understand the patient but not to impose their feelings and counterreactions.

This begins to reveal my stance. I am a mainstream contemporary analyst. I cannot think of myself as a one-person analyst because I am so very much in the room with my patients emotionally as well as physically, interacting even when silent. Silence is not an analytic virtue in its own right, but is sometimes needed to give the patient space that the analyst does not fill with talk because of her own anxiety, discomfort with the silence, or need to reveal. I do not use silence unfeelingly, as the stereotype would suggest. In fact, I talk quite a lot, but always in a considered way. This is analogous to thought as trial action.

To think before one speaks is the opposite of unfeeling. It respects the patient and the process. I consider whether what I am saying is in the best interest of the patient. The so-called two-person analyst may argue that he, too, functions in the best interest of the patient by making self-revelations. This may turn out to be an irreconcilable difference.

I feel happy when I know that the patient and I have made a momentary connection by "touching"—that is, by feeling the same affect at the same time, triggered by what the patient is telling me. My life experience enables me to understand and feel the patient's affect, but the resonance is with the life story and affect of the patient, not with mine. I think it would be counterproductive to reveal whence in my past or present life my responses arise.

The thrust of this book is mainstream theory brought up-to-date. Yes, theory construction has continued after Freud, continues to this very day, and will continue into the future. In that sense it is no longer valid to speak of *Freudian,* or *classical,* or *traditional* theory, but rather *psychoanalytic developmental psychology*—that is, *mainstream* theory with addenda provided by contemporary theorists.

It is a cumulative theory. The child observationalists (Emde 1980, 1988a,b, 1999, Osofsky 1979), in particular, are extending our knowledge about early development. Their work would hardly be possible without the pioneering contributions of the ego psychologists as their base. To illustrate: Heinz Hartmann built on Freud; René A. Spitz built on Freud and Hartmann; and Robert N. Emde is currently building on Freud, Hartmann, and Spitz. The new information does not replace basic theory, although it inevitably alters some by extension and eliminates that which has become obsolete. As it accumulates, it will be richer tomorrow than it is today.

I like *mainstream* as a metaphor. The Ohio River, as it flows into the Mississippi, contributes 50 percent to the waters of the mainstream, forming a larger and qualitatively different river. *Mainstream* better conveys the flow of theory construction than designations such as *classical* or *traditional.* Within it one can show which tributaries contribute to the mainstream, which flow away and detract, and which have dried up and are no longer of more than historical interest. It also helps in the evaluation of new proposals. Some streams flow away from the mainstream, taking mainstream waters away with them.

The most important tributary to flow into the mainstream is ego psychology. It began in the 1940s as one of the several offshoots of the structural theory. It represents the major contribution to theory construction after Freud. Now it has merged with the mainstream and is no longer a stand-alone theory. An example is *separation-individuation.* In earlier writings, whenever this concept was mentioned, it called for reference to Mahler and colleagues (1975). Now authors use the concept without attribution. This is not a reflection on their scholarship; rather, it illustrates how ego psychology has mingled with the mainstream and has enhanced it. *Psychoanalytic developmental psychology,* then, refers to mainstream psychoanalysis—Freud's basic theories enriched by ego psychology to form a merged theory greater than the sum of its parts.

In 1972 we (Blanck and Blanck) said: "The propulsive power of the structural theory is such that we have yet to see the end of its enormous potential for theory construction. After almost fifty years, its thrust still extends far into the future" (p. 668). We did not then fully appreciate how prophetic that was.

This book summarizes the findings of the first-generation ego psychologists—Freud, Hartmann, Jacobson, Spitz, and

Mahler—on the nature of structure, on psychoanalytic object relations theory, on transference, and on diagnosis, and, to illuminate the theory and technique, presents a case and recommends the most desirable form of treatment, which for this patient is psychoanalysis. In a bow to pragmatism, it shall also show how to treat this same patient when treatment has to be curtailed for extraneous reasons. Where possible, I shall illustrate with patient–therapist dialogue.

Finally, emboldened by the fulfillment of our 1972 prediction, I shall venture to predict the future direction of theory construction.

1

Art and Science

The theory of psychoanalysis is a science, although some philosophers of science dispute this because, they contend, psychoanalysis does not meet some of the criteria of the "hard" sciences, especially the criteria of replicability and measurement. In a sense they are correct. Once patients are analyzed, they are changed and cannot be reanalyzed all over again, nor are there accurate instruments for measurement of gain. Patients who have been analyzed do sometimes return for more analysis. Often referred to as reanalysis, this is a misnomer; they can only be additionally analyzed.

The argument about replicability is fallacious. Other sciences, too, are accepted as such even though their observations cannot be replicated. Astronomy, for example, deals with events as they occur in the universe that cannot be replicated in the laboratory.

How Can Psychoanalysis Be Proven, Then?

The data of psychoanalysis are derived from two sources. Freud's method was to use his clinical experience in the treatment of adults. This is still valid. What has been added is child observation. We now enjoy the benefit of deriving data from both the couch and from the work of the child observationalists. Much of what I shall be discussing will be the combined theory derived from clinical study of adults and the relatively newer discoveries about development by means of child observation.

How Do We Apply It?

Although the theory is a science, the application of psychoanalytic theory to the treatment situation, whether that be psychoanalysis proper or psychoanalytically informed psychotherapy, is an art.

The talent possessed by an artist is the ability to dip into the primary process and to recover, using the raw material from the primary process to create something communicable. Kris (1952) described this process as regression (to the primary process) "in the service of the ego," by which he meant that the recovery is an essential part of the artistic creation. The artist derives raw material from the primary process and shapes the raw material into something communicable, resulting in a work of art. Regression to the primary process without recovery in the service of the ego results in smearing, not art.

This is dramatically illustrated at the Antwerp Museum where there are some of Van Gogh's late works. One can see his deterioration into psychosis, as the paintings are displayed in chronological order. The very late paintings are mere smearings lacking communication to the viewer.

What Is the Art of the Therapist?

We tend not to think about the therapist as an artist. We are more likely to speak about the practice of medicine as an art. In medicine, good physicians use their talent combined with their knowledge in a creative way that is unique for a given patient. In psychoanalysis or psychoanalytically oriented psychotherapy, what analysts say, how we choose our words, and when we decide to intervene require knowledge of the theory and thoughtful application. Therapists and analysts have an especially tuned ear, sometimes referred to as a third ear. We hear the patients' verbalizations not only as they are conveyed manifestly, but by listening for the latent content, and by using ourselves, our analyzed unconscious, to hear the material in depth. Having been analyzed ourselves, we use what has been stirred up in us—called countertransference—to better understand the patient.

We mold the material, think about when and how to use it, even about how it contributes to the end goal of the treatment. These processes require that we dip into our own unconscious, and then recover from that regression in the service of our professional egos with thoughts that serve the patient. Then, at the appropriate time, we communicate it.

What Is Latent Content?

The patient makes statements that have both manifest and latent meanings. We are accustomed, in ordinary conversation, to listen to the manifest content only—in other words, to exactly what the person is saying consciously. This is a good thing. In our ordinary relationships, there is no need to listen for underlying meanings. Indeed, it would play havoc with any relationship to do so.

In the treatment situation, however, we do need to listen carefully to the underlying meaning of what the patient is saying. That kind of listening is in itself an art. As a simple example, the patient says, "I do not want to be here." If the therapist were to take that at face value, she might say, "So why have you come?" That would be a mistake that is likely to drive the patient away. The therapist thinks to herself, "But he is here. He came of his own free will. How and when can I use that underlying knowledge to help him?"

The Art of Phrasing and Timing

Notice that the above therapist thought of two things—how and when. The how deals, of course, with what to say. This frightens beginners unnecessarily. Perhaps in no other practice is it unimportant that the therapist use precisely the right words as long as the intervention is correct. This can be quite reassuring. The therapist who speaks to the patient correctly does the right thing regardless of whether the wording is elegant. Elegance comes with experience. It is part of the art, but not an essential part.

Timing is also important. The therapist has to think of when to make an intervention, and timing is probably more important than proper wording. The right time is when the patient's verbalizations have entered the preconscious and added up to something interpretable.

What Do We Mean by Communication?

Communication is a feature of object relations (see Chapter 5). The artist, whether painter, writer, musician, or actor, must be aware of an audience. The therapist has only the patient as audience. But what the therapist communicates is vital to the patient's therapeutic progress.

Therapy as Art

That therapy is an art does not mean that anything goes, anymore than is true for any artist. There are rules to be followed. In psychoanalytic therapy, the theory defines the rules. Some free spirits who overvalue their intuition undervalue theory. I am advocating playing by the rules. An exceptionally gifted musician, artist, or analyst can take some risks, but those come only after the artist has been trained to follow the rules. Most of us cannot take risks. It may hurt our narcissism to have to think of ourselves as unexceptional, yet it is best for the patient that we remain disciplined.

Analogy with Other Arts

I heard a famous musician declare that the era of romanticism is over. Yet we still hear music from that era and even from the baroque, while contemporary music is being developed. Musicologists agree that contemporary music could not have sprung full blown without the influence of all that preceded it.

This may be said of the "hard" sciences as well as of art. Would we have modern physics without Newton? And it applies particularly to psychoanalysis because it is part science and part art. In addition to the treatment situation, we have other artistic applications of psychoanalytic theory—literature and drama being the best known of these.

Are There Really New Theories?

Scientific curiosity impels us to look at new theories. We are also impelled, indeed required, to be discriminating about them. It is my contention that the "new" theories in psychoanalysis are not new. We all stand on Freud's shoulders. It is true that some of his ideas have to be discarded. The prime example of that is his female psychology, because he was altogether wrong about it. But there is no would-be stand-alone theory that does not have its roots somewhere in Freud's work. The roots of behavior modification, for example, lie in Freud's recommendation that the phobic patient be exposed to that which she fears.

We can trace similar connections for cognitive, relational, interpersonal, self psychology, British object relations theory, and other theories. Object relations, in particular, permeates Freud's work from as early as 1902. Clearly, any "new" object relations theory derives from Freud.

What Theory Shall We Use Now?

If the art in therapy lies in the disciplined application of theory, what theory shall we apply? There are many choices as new theories proliferate. Some have substance; some are fads that will pass. The "new" theories that may be traced to their roots in classical psychoanalytic theory can only be regarded as partial theories. It is more useful to regard them as extensions of Freud's thoughts, and then to examine them to evaluate whether they extend in a useful direction.

Is Psychoanalytic Developmental Theory New?

No. Newness for its own sake has no value. Psychoanalytic developmental theory extends psychoanalysis without discarding its main tenets. That extension required the contributions of ego psychology to provide a developmental stance. Developmental theory is largely an addendum to already existing theory, the logical next step after Freud's introduction of the structural theory.

What Is the Structural Theory?

Freud revised some of his own work as he gained clinical experience. In 1923 in *The Ego and the Id* he announced his discovery that part of the ego is unconscious. That was a turning point in psychoanalytic theory construction. He proposed a tri-partite theory—the psyche no longer consists only of ego and id; there is a superego as well. And the ego, heretofore believed to be synonymous with consciousness, was found to be partly unconscious.

This was a radical and seminal turn in theory construction. A new pathway was opened for further theory construction. The newly discovered unconscious ego and superego intrigued a new generation of theorists with the possibilities of exploring the qualities and functions of these agencies.

Heinz Hartmann, known as the father of ego psychology, took the structural theory toward expanding psychoanalysis into a psychology of normality as well as pathology by introducing new ideas about both the conscious and unconscious parts of the ego.

In addition to Hartmann, the principal first generation of ego psychologists consists of his collaborators—Ernst Kris and Rudolph Loewenstein, Edith Jacobson, René A. Spitz, and Margaret S. Mahler. These are the theorists who built the bridge to the psychoanalytic developmental psychology that we are discussing here.

Why Have I Chosen Certain Theorists?

Their findings are internally consistent. By integrating them (Blanck and Blanck 1974), we arrive at a cohesive theory that dominated psychoanalytic thinking in the post–World War II era and now has made its way into contemporary theory.

A number of theorists, some of whose work I admire and use in my teaching and clinical work, are not part of the original ego psychologists, but follow after them. A case in point is Hans

Loewald (1980), who wrote about the therapeutic action of psychoanalysis, about ego organization, about the resolution of the Oedipus complex, and more.

What Was New about Ego Psychology?

The newness in ego psychology lay in its direction. It called attention to the vicissitudes of life before the oedipal crisis. That became possible as Hartmann and his collaborators found ego functions not heretofore recognized because Freud had not studied early life. He thought that neurosis revolves around the oedipal crisis, the core conflict, and that is what requires analytic attention. This is still held to be true, but so much more has been added, as we have now come to realize that there is life before the oedipal period and that early life influences how the oedipal conflict takes shape (G. Blanck 1984).

How Do I Define Psychoanalytic Developmental Psychology?

Developmental theory has not been defined clearly enough, leaving room for it to mean different things to different people. Because of its roots in ego psychology, and because some still believe that ego psychology is a theory of conscious deployment of ego functions, an erroneous assumption is in the air. Therefore, I reiterate that the very existence of ego psychology rests on Freud's discovery that part of the ego is unconscious.

Developmental theory, then, is basic psychoanalytic theory, plus the addenda of the ego psychologists, evolved now into a theory broader than both. One of its outstanding contributions is that it uncovers the heretofore hidden vicissitudes of the first days, weeks, months, and years of early life. In so doing, it provides the clinician with a way of understanding the patient in depth—the depth of her developmental vicissitudes as well as the depth of the unconscious. It retains all that is of value in classical psychoanalytic theory and enlarges it by absorbing ego psychology to become a theory of normality as well as pathology.

Why Is Ego Psychology a Misnomer?

The would-be stand-alone theories have titles, such as self psychology, lending themselves to the mistaken belief that they are theories unto themselves. It is necessary to emphasize that ego psychology is not an entire psychology, but, as I have indicated, a tributary of mainstream theory. The term *ego psychology*, then, is a misnomer in that it lends itself to misunderstanding of its place in the evolution of theory construction. Also, by adhering to Freud's early thoughts about the ego without consideration for the fact that he altered them in 1923, some misunderstand ego psychology to be a psychology of consciousness. For purposes of clarity, therefore, I believe that the designation *psychoanalytic developmental psychology* more precisely reflects that ego psychology is, in fact, a subtheory, a part of a larger whole.

How Does Developmental Psychology Expand Theory?

Basic Freudian theory presented us with a theory of psychosexual maturation. We spoke then of pregenital life and its conflicts. Developmental theory adds consideration of preoedipal life as well. This is not hair splitting even though those two periods of life coincide in time. Pregenital refers to the drives, while preoedipal refers to the object relations feature of the same developmental phase of life.

Another Example of Expansion

Edith Jacobson (1964) added developmental considerations to the theory of psychosexual maturation. She showed that the experiences of the self in interaction with the object consists of more than zonal gratification only. Using the feeding experience as an example, she highlighted that it consists of more than nourishment alone. The infant being fed experiences maternal touching, holding, babbling, and the like. Development takes place within the context of that total dyadic experience.

Knowledge about Early Life

The developmentalists are concerned with how the vicissitudes of early life form character, form patterning of object relations, and influence the direction in which the individual will develop. Spitz (1959) showed that deviant development at one phase skews development at the next phases. These patterns are reflected in the transference. In fact, the very definition of transference is the repetition of self and object relations patterns displaced from past to present (see Chapter 6). Behavior, affect, and attitudes in the transference reveal the forgotten experiences of early life—the time of life that is regarded as unrememberable because of infantile amnesia and unforgettable because it engraves the self with ineradicable storage of self and object experience that resides in the representational world. This is broader than the pre–ego psychological definition of transference. That was restricted to feelings and attitudes that are repressed, but rememberable when revived in the transference.

Where Does This Get Us?

This gives us a theory that enables the therapist to understand how and why the patient got the way she is. Then adaptive arrangements may be retained, while those that have become maladaptive may be shown to be needed no longer. This theory broadens the psychoanalytic process as both patient and analyst explore the very inception of the patient's developmental history in addition to the neurotic conflicts that were the sole interest of the early psychoanalysts.

This discussion exemplifies what I mean by theory construction as accrual. It does not imply that all that went before is to be retained. Theory is subject to reconsideration, weeding out, and revision as knowledge about human development expands.

2

The History
of Psychoanalytic
Developmental
Psychology

In diagnosing and treating patients, developmentalists take the historical route. They are interested not only in how their patients seem as they appear before them, but what in their life histories contributed to how they are today. I take a parallel route here in tracing the history of the theory. We understand it more thoroughly when we know whence it came, what is still regarded as valid, what has been added, and what has become obsolete.

Freud guarded the fragile new theory he was discovering by exercising paternal discipline on his followers. Now some theorists advocate pluralism, an all-encompassing attitude that permits many theories that Freud might have rejected to remain under the umbrella of the mainstream psychoanalytic organizations. But should a social phenomenon necessitated by the diverse populations be stretched to influence science? Although the politics and sociology of pluralism are beyond my scope here, I do question whether political correctness is to be applied to theory.

The Pre-psychoanalytic Era

Freud began his work in the late nineteenth century. He was then a neurologist who learned, while studying in Paris under the famous French neurologist Charcot, that hysterical paralysis was caused by forgotten (repressed) memories, usually of a sexual nature. Retrieval of these memories by means of hypnosis ostensibly cured the paralysis. Upon his return to Vienna, Freud began to practice what he had learned. Under hypnosis, patients recalled forgotten memories and, in many cases, the paralysis was dramatically cured.

Freud soon found, however, that hypnosis has its shortcomings. For one thing, not all patients can be hypnotized. Even among those who could, memories were not uniformly recalled. Moreover, in many cases the cure was temporary. After a brief remission the paralysis returned or was replaced by another symptom.

It is interesting to note that some of the simple psychologies are now advocating that a recall of a traumatic memory constitutes a cure. The fallacy is that a pathology is not created by a single memory, even one that is traumatic. Memories build, one upon the other; an earlier event becoming telescoped and compounded by a later one and all is woven into a single memory (Kris 1956a). And hardly ever is an event recalled exactly as it occurred. Even where there is corroboration by another person, we are hearing only how that person experienced it. The patient with whom we are dealing will have processed the experience according to her developmental pattern—the level of object relations that obtained, the degree of structuralization, and the affective state.

Freud abandoned hypnosis and tried to encourage memory by gently exerting pressure on the patient's forehead. This, too, had its limitations. He discovered free association shortly after that. The patient is instructed to say whatever comes to mind without censure or consideration for logical sequence. By this method, material in the unconscious is brought into the preconscious. We might say that this is the place where psychoanalysis proper began.

What Is the Unconscious?

The sine qua non of psychoanalytic theory is that there is an unconscious. No theory can claim to be psychoanalytic that disregards the unconscious. In the prepsychoanalytic era, it was known that memories and fantasies were forgotten. That there is an unconscious tells us where these memories and unconscious fantasies "reside." I am describing constructs, and the quotation marks connote that there is no physical locus for the unconscious. The concept is merely part of the construction of a theory around which analysts may organize their thoughts.

Early Topography

The discovery of the unconscious led to a simple topographic theory—conscious and unconscious. This was destined to become more elaborate later on when the idea of a preconscious was added. Now it consists of three layers: conscious, preconscious, and unconscious.

What Is the Preconscious?

The preconscious is a halfway "place" where memories and fantasies that were unconscious are elicited in the course of treatment. Then they are closer to consciousness than before, but not quite conscious yet. This idea exerts an important influence on technique. When material is in the preconscious, it may be brought into consciousness by an interpretation.

What Is an Interpretation?

An interpretation is a statement of what is in the preconscious—a defense mechanism behind which lies a fantasy, a wish. The analyst enables the patient to bring that material there by dealing first with the defense that keeps the material unconscious. When it comes into the preconscious, either analyst or patient may make the interpretation. One of the contributions of ego psychology to modern practice is that it is often more desirable that the patient arrive at the interpretation (Kris 1956b) because one of the objectives of modern psychoanalysis is to promote separation and independence. Interpretation is one form of intervention.

What Is an Intervention?

Intervention is the generic term under which interpretation is subsumed. This definition leaves room for the analyst or therapist to make other statements that are not interpretations—to ask questions, to make observations, to ask the patient to clarify, to make comments, to keep the flow of associations going. Not everything the analyst says, therefore, is an interpretation. We are better served if we limit the definition of interpretation rather than spreading it loosely to cover everything the analyst says.

What Is the Superego?

Freud defined superego as a differentiated grade within the ego. He thought that the ego arises out of the id and the superego out of the ego. When they are not in conflict, ego and superego are one.

What Is Conflict Theory?

Psychoanalytic theory was a conflict theory from the beginning. But since 1923 it has become more elaborate than before. In conflict, a compromise is effected to satisfy both agencies. This can result in symptom formation. Sometimes symptoms are rather obscure, such as compulsive behavior that verges on normal orderliness.

What Is Anxiety?

At first Freud thought of anxiety in chemical terms. Anxiety was caused by toxins, the result of dammed up libido—that is, absence of discharge of sexual substances. We refer to this as Freud's first theory of anxiety.

After the introduction of the structural theory, Freud had to revise his first theory of anxiety because the concept of a tripartite structure made the matter more complex. The second theory of anxiety is no longer a toxic theory. It deals with anxiety as the affect that results from conflict. The competent ego of the neurotic experiences anxiety as a signal to employ defense mechanisms and negotiate a compromise.

We know more about the borderline conditions since approximately 1950. The ego of the borderline patient is less competent and therefore less able to employ defense mechanisms. As I shall show in Chapter 12, the borderline ego defends differently.

What Is a Defense?

The compromise, although designed to relieve anxiety, is not totally effective. That is why the ego has to defend against the residual anxiety. Anna Freud (1936) described the defensive function of the ego. She enumerated many, but not all, defense mechanisms, such as repression, regression, reaction-formation, reversal, denial, projection, turning against the self, and identification with the aggressor. This does not exhaust the list. One of the most prominent defense mechanisms in highly intelligent patients is intellectualization. Heinz Hartmann (1958) proposed that, in addition to the defensive function of the ego, there is also an adaptive function (see Chapter 3).

What Is Dream Theory?

In *The Interpretation of Dreams* (1900), Freud described "the stuff that dreams are made on." The dream contains recent material—known as the day residue—plus a childhood memory and a wish. Freud showed that the logic in dreams is not the Aristotelian logic that we use in waking life. Dreams employ the primary process, our primitive way of thinking. He also demonstrated how to understand the construction of a dream by dealing with each element. His purpose was to propound dream theory. We do not analyze dreams in that way for treatment purposes. We select those elements of a dream that will propel the treatment.

Freud regarded the dream as the royal road to the unconscious. That still holds, but now we do not always take the royal road. One reason is that treatment has a more profound purpose than simply to make the unconscious conscious. We still want to uncover repressed memories and unconscious fantasies, but we are also concerned with self and object relations (see Chapter 5) and with adaptation (see Chapter 3).

Also, we now better understand that not all patients are neurotic. In some borderline cases, where the defensive function of the ego is less competent than in neurosis, the objective is to strengthen the ego and thereby the defensive function. Especially in low-level borderline cases, repression may be insufficient. There, rather than making the unconscious conscious, the therapeutic objective is the reverse—to aid repression. I shall have more to say about the borderline conditions in Chapter 12.

What Is the Primary Process?

We have two thought processes, primary and secondary. The primary process has a logic of its own that uses condensation, representing two or more events as one. It employs depicting a part of something or someone to represent the whole (*pars pro toto*), it uses symbols to disguise, and it censors unacceptable (to the ego) thoughts, affects, fantasies, and wishes.

What Is the Secondary Process?

This is the way we normally think in our waking state unless we are severely disturbed. Infants and psychotics think in the primary process. Developmentally, as the child's world begins to become organized somewhere toward the end of the first year of life and during the second year, a transition to the secondary process is made. Thought becomes more orderly and follows Aristotelian laws of logic. This shift is noticeable in the second year of life when the child employs rituals in the service of keeping things in order.

Infantile Sexuality

Freud discovered infantile sexuality in 1905. This caused him great problems with his colleagues and with the general medical community. They could not accept that infants and children are sexual beings. Child observation leaves no doubt that sexuality is active in infantile life (Galenson and Roiphe 1976).

The Libido Theory

Early psychoanalytic theory used the concept of libido to account for the flow of energy. Freud proposed a sort of developmental theory that we now term psychosexual progression. Libido flows from one physical zone to another. At first it is fixated in the mouth, by the second year of life it flows to the anus, and still later to the phallus. This describes the well-known psychosexual progression from oral to anal to phallic.

The Dual-Drive Theory

It was not until 1920 that Freud, finding a single-drive theory inadequate, proposed that there is a second drive. He termed the newly discovered drive *Thanatos* and renamed the libidinal drive *Eros*. To him, Thanatos is equated with a death instinct, by which he meant that all organic matter is driven to return to the inorganic state.

Although the dual-drive theory is still used today, it is much modified. Many, perhaps most, psychoanalysts do not adhere to a death instinct, although they accept that there are the two drives—libido and aggression. There is also controversy about how these are defined.

We have less trouble with libido than with aggression. Partly, this is explained by the fact that aggression was tacked on to drive theory some twenty years after the proposal of the libido theory. It was assumed that it follows the same vicissitudes as libido, but this is uncertain.

In his later, posthumously published work in 1940, Freud redefined the drives and their functions. Libido, he said, is the force that seeks union. Aggression is the force that seeks to separate and thus destroy.

This has important implications for the theory I am expounding, which deals with union and separation, using the two drives alternately and in unison. Development takes place in sequences of differentiation and integration. Differentiation at one level leads to a new configuration that proceeds to integrate at a next higher level, then again to a higher level of differentiation and integration. I shall have more to say about this when I discuss the work of the ego psychologists (Chapter 3).

The Aggressive Drive

We are left with different theories about the aggressive drive. Since it was tacked on long after Freud proposed libido theory, it is an open question whether it follows the same course. There is even a difference about its origin. Most theorists accept Freud's assertion that aggression arises out of the id. Jacobson (1964) suggests that both drives develop independently after birth. The theories help us understand how drive energy propels development. It is especially useful to think, as Freud suggested, that libido serves union and aggression serves separation because developmental theory is so involved with integration and differentiation. It also enables us to think of the aggressive drive as not altogether destructive, but as serving growth by powering differentiation.

Interim Theories

In the period between 1900 and 1923, Freud worked prodigiously on several matters, such as narcissism, depression, and group psychology. His paper "On Narcissism" (1914), was intended as an introduction, but he never completed it. In modern theory, narcissism plays a rather large role, but the theory has been much revised and amended. We now think that narcissism can be healthy if both self and object representations are regarded equally. Or it can be pathological if there is an imbalance in either direction. I shall return to this subject later.

Freud also wrote some philosophical papers such as "Moses and Monotheism" and "Civilization and Its Discontents." There is reason to think that Freud's interim theoretical writings, valuable as they are, would benefit from reconsideration and revision in the light of the structural theory.

The Case Histories

Freud wrote five case histories. He had treated three of these patients—Dora, a patient he diagnosed as hysteric with somatic symptoms; "A Case of Obsessional Neurosis," nicknamed the Rat Man; and "A Case of Infantile Neurosis," nicknamed the Wolf Man. He also helped the father of a child, Little Hans, analyze the boy but did not treat him directly, and he wrote an analysis of a paranoid patient, Schreber, from reading the memoirs that Schreber wrote while he was confined to a mental institution.

These case histories are now of historical interest. We can follow Freud's gropings as he sought to discover a theory of neurosis through them. The histories have been reviewed in the light of modern theory. It is questionable whether Dora, an adolescent, should have been treated as an adult, whether the father of Little Hans could be his analyst, and whether the Rat Man and the Wolf Man were truly neurotic. However, we learn much about paranoia from Freud's study of Schreber's memoirs.

What Is the Place of Ego Psychology?

Ego psychology was never a separate theory. It was spoken of that way for heuristic purpose as it was being developed. But it was always considered to be a part of the entirety of psychoanalytic theory. In reviewing Hartmann's clinical notes, it was found that he was very much a mainstream psychoanalyst (Dunn, personal communication 1999). I have described how ego psychology is now merged with the mainstream. I shall describe ego psychology in more detail in the next chapter.

3

Ego Psychology:
The Tributary

Ego psychology begins with Freud's introduction of the structural theory in 1923. Several theorists took off from there in a number of different directions, such as exploration of the ego in psychosis (P. Federn), the ego in interpersonal interaction (H. S. Sullivan), and the ego in conflict (M. Klein). The direction I shall follow here leads to Hartmann's introduction of ego psychology proper in 1939 (translated into English in 1958) and Anna Freud's description of the defensive function of the ego in 1936. I will not present an exhaustive summary of these theorists' work, but rather restrict myself to the major aspects to show how their contributions and those of his collaborators constitute a point of departure for the ego psychologists who followed after.

The Contribution of Anna Freud

As noted, the theoretical thrust that the structural theory propelled was exploration of the unconscious part of the ego. Anna Freud focused her study on a major aspect of the unconscious ego—the defensive function. She described how defense operates and enumerated a few of the defensive functions such as repression, regression, isolation, reaction-formation, and reversal. She included sublimation, about which we still remain uncertain, questioning whether it is a defense mechanism or a normal redirection of the drives.

The Contribution of Heinz Hartmann

Hartmann introduced the idea that there is an adaptive function of the ego and proceeded to explore it. His theory begins with the encounter of the neonate with the mothering person, who is the neonate's environment. Hartmann defined adaptation as a reciprocal relationship between the organism and its environment. Adaptation is the neonate's first postnatal task. Hartmann assumed that the neonate is uniquely endowed with an adaptive capacity. There is no time to lose. The neonate must breathe at once and then suck in order to survive. Infant and mother must find a way of fitting together, which Hartmann regarded as of overriding importance. In describing adaptation, Hartmann turned psychoanalysis from a psychopathology only into a psychology of normal development as well.

To explain how these inborn or innate capacities exist, Hartmann proposed that there is an undifferentiated matrix that contains the ego, id, adaptive capacity, and the developmental timetable. The undifferentiated matrix may be likened to Mendelaeff's periodic table, which leaves space for elements as yet undiscovered. So it is with the undifferentiated matrix. It contains all that is innately endowed and allows for differentiation after birth. Ego and id differentiate after birth. Functions such as walking and talking develop according to a maturational timetable. Jacobson (1964) added that the two drives are also merged within the matrix and have to differentiate. We (Blanck and Blanck 1974) suggested that the affects also have to differentiate. Thus, some functions differentiate immediately upon birth, and some such as walking await physical maturation.

A basic tenet of Hartmann's theory is that development is a continuing process of differentiation and integration. Differentiation takes place at one level, leading to integration of ever broadening function combined with experience at a next higher level, only to differentiate and then integrate once again at a still higher level. This idea appears rather abstract until we note that the child observationalists, Mahler and Spitz, saw how the child uses separation and return to mother for "refueling" and then to separate again.

Another aspect of adaptation is the elaboration of automatisms. To conserve energy, the steps leading up to an action that is to be repeated need not be taken anew each time, but become automatic. This applies in particular to thinking processes.

Structure formation also serves adaptation. Identifications reflect the continuity of relationship to parental figures. Thus the superego, the result of identification with the parents, is an outcome of adaptation.

Hartmann wrote also about other features of adaptation: object relations, intelligence, rationality, thinking, maintenance of equilibrium. And with his collaborators, Ernst Kris and Rudolph M. Loewenstein, he examined genetic factors—how early and possibly even outdated experience still exerts an influence on present-day functioning. They also considered matters such as aggression, superego formation, the place of theory in psychoanalysis, and the technique of interpretation.

The Contribution of Edith Jacobson

Jacobson's contributions exerted a major influence on psychoanalytic developmental psychology. Her concept of mental representation establishes that there is an internal world where experience, images of self and object, and the interrelationship between these images reside. As the infant gathers experience that is affectively charged, he internalizes representations of those experiences. To simplify this, think of the neonate's encounter with the mothering person as leaving a lasting impression in the mind or psyche of the child. The representational world is the "place" where those impressions register. That registration is not the mother as she is in reality, but the impression of her that the child acquires, heavily influenced by the affect that accompanies the experience. We may liken this to photography as an art form. If the photographer wishes to use that medium as art, he does not attempt to capture reality on film, but adjusts his focus to depict an impression that he wishes to convey. Another person may look at the object he has photographed and see something else. Each child acquires unique representations based on unique affective experience.

In this context Jacobson was able also to elaborate upon the establishment of self and object relations. Her work is far ranging, touching matters such as depression and other affective experiences. She is considered to be the immediate theoretical heir and elaborator of that which was begun by Hartmann. She showed how adaptation leads to establishment of the self and self representations within the experience of adequate mothering.

Child Observation

The child observationalists Spitz and Mahler have given us guidelines so that we know the parameters of normal development and can examine what deviations from the normal might prevail in a given case. Thus we have a tool for evaluating the probable effect on development of certain events in the patient's history.

Are These Not Mere Assumptions?

Yes and no. The child observation studies have established the features of early development and are not assumptions according to their data. As applied to a given case, however, much does have to be assumed because there we are dealing with an unrememberable period of the patient's life. The surest pathway to an approximation of what early life may have been like for an adult patient is his behavior in the transference.

We combine the guidelines provided by the child observationalists with ascertainment of the level of object relations in the transferential behavior. These provide opportunities for hypothesizing. Hypotheses need to be tested in the clinical situation and must be discarded in the face of additional information that changes the direction of our thinking.

Therefore, a hypothesis provides the therapist with a direction to follow until it is proven. The therapist has to be ready to discard it and to change course if it seems to be incorrect. If hypotheses are rigidly held, they can carry the treatment in the wrong direction.

How Can We Know Whether a Hypothesis Is Correct?

Treatment must be mutative. One way of knowing whether the treatment moves on is production of new material. New material is confirmatory. Dreams may sometimes be confirmatory. Although patients do not get better in a straight line, improvement tells us that we are on the right track.

The Contribution of René A. Spitz

Spitz was one of the two child observationalists who opened the way to understanding early life, the period that has so often been described as unrememberable and unforgettable. He showed how the ego, at first barely distinguishable from the id, becomes organized by means of affective experience. He found that there are three levels of organization, each with an indicator that informs us that organization has indeed been achieved in accordance with a developmental timetable.

The child first organizes the gestalt of the human face because she experiences the appearance of a face in conjunction with relief from hunger and other discomforts. After repeatedly experiencing relief, the neonate begins to smile at the face. The smile is the first indicator that a level of organization has taken place. That organization is limited to the experience itself, plus the configuration of the human face—eyes, nose, and mouth full face and in motion. The child will not smile at a profile or a still face.

Several months later the child no longer smiles at all faces. She has become able to distinguish a familiar from a strange face and withdraws from the stranger. Some children cry at the sight of a stranger, some simply tense their bodies. This so-called stranger anxiety is the indicator that a second level of organization has taken place. The child has established the mother as "the libidinal object proper."

The indicator of the third level of organization is semantic communication. At approximately 18 months the child begins to speak, especially to say no. This is a sign that she has become separate enough as an individual realize that the mother is not part of the self and may be refused. Speech is also a sign not only of higher organization of self and object relations but of the realization that one deals with another person across a chasm of separateness. No longer can the child expect that the mother will respond to her wishes automatically; the mother has to be told what the child wants. Spitz designated this level of organization as acquisition of semantic communication because it transcends speech; it communicates to another person. It represents a new level of object relations.

I discussed communication in Chapter 2, where I described true art as something that communicates. The understanding that this is a necessity in dealing with other persons underpins all of our later relationships.

The Contribution of Margaret S. Mahler

Mahler began her studies with psychotic children. She took a turn into investigating normality by using the observational method to study infants and toddlers and their relationships with parents. The major form of her study is of mother–child pairs in the first three years of life. Out of that study she was able to deduce that psychological birth—the acquisition of a distinct and separate identity—takes place approximately three years after physical birth.

She describes in detail how the neonate, at first in a state of merger with the mothering person, gradually separates and individuates to become a person in her own right. Mahler found four different phases of this three-year-long separation-individuation process. The first is differentiation, when the child begins to experience herself as somewhat separate from the mother. When physical maturation enables the child to crawl and then walk, she enters the practicing subphase of the separation-individuation process. Mahler describes this subphase as one of discovery and mastery. It has been called the child's love affair with the world.

The world expands and the child feels elation as she discovers new things and new physical skills.

After a while reality testing sets in and the child experiences anxiety as she begins to realize that she is a very small person in a very large world. She needs to return to home base, a process that Mahler termed rapprochement. The role the mother plays is of greater importance than meets the eye as the child seeks reassurance that home base is still there. Mahler regarded this subphase as crucial to the child's further development and entry into the larger world.

If it goes smoothly, the child is on the way to object constancy, a process that goes on for an unlimited time. If the mother is less than receptive to the child's need to return for one more reassurance, further development is retarded. Mahler even suggested that rapprochement disappointment makes for incomplete separation-individuation and thereby predisposes to a borderline rather than a fully structured condition.

Although Hartmann defined adaptation as a reciprocal relationship between the organism and its environment, Mahler found that that relationship is not equal. It is the infant who plays the larger role, because at birth the child is in a high state of adaptiveness. The mother lends herself to it, but does not bring an equal capacity for adaptation. This takes much burden off the mothering person, whose role is limited by the child's innate endowment, especially the capacity to adapt and to extract from the environment. I have extrapolated from this discovery to propose that it is useful even in the treatment of adults, and I have advocated a technical stance that conforms with it.

I have sketched out the basic tenets of ego psychology. For a more detailed study of the subject I suggest the original sources. For a more detailed secondary source, see Blanck and Blanck 1974.

4

The Nature of Structure

In the early years of theory construction, structure was thought to consist of id and ego. When Freud discovered that part of the ego is unconscious, a third element of structure—superego—was added. Hartmann's and Jacobson's attention to the concept of the representational world (further elaborated by Sandler and Rosenblatt 1952), made room for more than the three psychic agencies in the configuration that we now call structure. Now the patterning of the self representation in its relationship with the object representations is added to the concept of structure. (This will be elaborated in Chapter 5.)

All of these concepts are regarded as constructs and could safely be said to reside within the unconscious part of the ego. Recent discoveries in the neurosciences, as I shall discsuss shortly, now suggest that there may be a physical alteration in the brain as the consequence of structure formation.

How Is Structure Formed?

Structure comes about in two ways that operate simultaneously: (1) with differentiation of ego and id, and superego formation;

and (2) with establishment of the internal world as the result of affectively tinged experiences of the self in interaction with the object. Interpersonal at first, images of these experiences become intrapsychic as internalization relegates them to the representational world. Structure, then, is an end product of differentiation and internalization.

What Is Affect?

Affective experience is the keystone of structure formation. Spitz (1972) suggested that there is a bond between affect and percept. Emde (1999), continuing Spitz's work, shows that affect is the element that maintains cohesion in the midst of the turmoil of developmental change. Thus, Emde adds to Hartmann's assertion that affects are adaptive by showing more precisely how they serve adaptation.

With Spitz's and Emde's work on affect theory we may now say that, from the beginning of life, the affects serve to bind the structure *in statu nascendi*. Affect may be likened to the warp in weaving, the thread that gives the pattern coherence. (Webster's Third International dictionary defines warp as the basic foundation or material of a structure.). This supports the assertion that the "talking cures" that include affective experience are more durable than the cognitive, behavioral, and psychopharmacological ones.

What Is Internalization?

Internalization is an "intaking" process that converts external experiences and situates them in the representational world. There are several such intaking processes—introjection, incorporation, identification, and the like. I regard *internalization* as the generic term under which these other processes are subsumed.

Internalization is central to the establishment of self and object relations patterning. Early in life, there is a turning point in development when the heretofore interpersonal interaction between child and mother becomes intrapsychic—that is, becomes internalized and relegated to the representational world.

What Is the Definition of Structure?

Structure consists of the enduring forms into which mental operations are organized. This restates that id, ego, and superego as well as the representational world, once established, constitute structure.

Where Are These Structures?

As constructs, they have no locus. But we have reason to think now that structures are more literal. Eric Kandel (1990), a neuroscientist, studied structuralization in a worm. He applied the same stimulus, an electrical current, repeatedly. Upon dissection he found thickening of the neuronal membrane, proof of registry of the repeated stimuli. Thus, current interest in the interface between psychoanalysis and the neurosciences includes investigation of the intertwining of the psychological with the physical aspects of structure formation. I shall have more to say about this in Chapter 15.

What Is the Origin of Structure?

Freud thought that the ego arises out of the id and that the superego, a differentiated grade within the ego, is the last agency of structure that develops as heir to the Oedipus complex. Hartmann differed with Freud on the origin of ego. Hartmann said that there is neither ego nor id at the beginning of life; these two agencies arise from the undifferentiated matrix after birth. In deciding which theory prevails, we are obliged to choose the one that serves theory construction better.

Why Does Origin of Ego Matter?

Development (referring to psychological growth) and maturation (referring to physical growth) both proceed within the mother–infant dyad. Spitz (1945) showed that infants deprived of maternal contact fail to develop and to mature. That proved that maternal stimulation quickens ego functions and promotes ego organization as well as physical maturation. Jacobson noted that development proceeds under the auspices of adequate mothering.

Hartmann's proposal that both ego and id derive from the undifferentiated matrix and differentiate after birth focuses attention on the mother–infant dyad. It enables us to study ego development as it takes place in the context of maternal stimulation We may then speculate that structure is organized into a constellation as smaller structures form into larger ones, with affect providing cohesion in the midst of change.

Thus, Hartmann's theory may replace Freud's because it is more seminal. It is a fork in the road of theory construction, taking theory in the direction of a developmental point of view. This theory opens pathways toward study of how the human infant and the mothering person interact and how that interaction promotes structuralization. It led the child observationalists toward their studies of infants and their mothers.

How Does Structure Grow out of Experience?

Consider that affective experiences, such as the complex one of being fed several times a day, become organized into a gestalt—hunger, cry, footsteps, appearance of a face, being held, interaction with the mothering person, relief from distress. It is the experience of these events, and more complex ones that occur later, with affect operating as the warp to provide cohesion, that becomes organized into structures.

How Is the Concept of Structure Expanded?

Now the concept of structure is expanded to include more than id, ego, superego, and the body image. It consists of registry of experiences that, for the human infant, are far more complex than the stimuli that Kandel applied to his worms. Nevertheless, the analogy is clear.

As these experiences are repeated they become predictable, because, we speculate, neuronal pathways are laid down, acquiring the status of a structure that has physiological consequence. We are still in the process of making the first bold steps in the direction of connecting the psychological with the physiological.

Can We Prove that Structures Exist?

It may take many years before we find a means to detect structures in the human brain, as was found in the simpler nervous system of the worm. For the time being, such proof is not available even upon autopsy. Is that because pathologists are not trained to look for them, or is the instrumentation we have today insufficiently refined, or both?

Can the Brain Be Altered?

It is not such a bold assertion to state that the brain is altered by experience. We already know from psychopharmacology that the brain can be altered chemically by introduction of a foreign substance. We may assume that affective experience alters not only the chemistry of the brain, but the physiology as well. The effect of chemical alteration ceases with withdrawal of the drug. I have said that affective experience in the course of life experience or in psychotherapy or psychoanalysis provides more enduring change because it is not dependent on the introduction of an extraneous substance such as a drug.

Are Representations Structures?

The answer has to be yes. The first images, even before they become stable representations, are of a merged self and object. With differentiation comes gradual psychic separation followed by integration on the next higher level. Simultaneously, self and object images become more and more distinct one from the other. Ultimately they stabilize; then we no longer refer to them as images that have a fleeting life, but as representations that possess stability.

What Value Does This Theory Have for the Treatment Situation?

Early experiences, fixed in the structure, determine the way the individual feels about self and others. If the self representation is of less value than the object representations, the patient will present with low self esteem. If the self representations are overvalued, the patient will exhibit a form of pathological narcissism.

How Does the Therapist Detect This?

Among its other functions, the transference provides a window to the internal structure. The patient who says, "One look at your face, Doctor, and I know that you can help me," is revealing overvaluation of the object representations. The patient who says, "My wife insists that I come to see you, but I think I know what to do without outside help," is displaying a form of pathological narcissism—imbalance of self and object representations in the direction of overvaluation of the self representations. There are other forms of pathological narcissism (Blanck and Blanck 1979). Healthy narcissism is defined by Jacobson (1964) as evenly distributed cathexis between self and object representations. These examples illustrate how the therapist listens and observes attitudes that reveal the internal structure. (For a more thorough discussion of transference, see Chapter 6.)

Can Structure Be Altered?

It has always been assumed that the very purpose of psychoanalytic treatment is to alter structure. Before ego psychology, it was the simple matter of altering the relationship among ego, id, and superego. The literature is rife with suggestions about strengthening the ego, modifying the superego, and taming the id. The ego is strengthened by analyzing conflict and thereby freeing psychic energy that was bound up in defense, thus enabling the ego to function relatively free of conflict. The overly harsh superego of the neurotic patient is modified by showing that childhood restraints are no longer adaptive. The id is tamed in a number of ways, especially by processing wishes through the ego, providing for thought as trial action, or, to put this another way, substituting judgment for impulsive action. Tripartite structural change used to be regarded as the end point of treatment. Matters are far more complex today because of the expanded view of what constitutes structure.

To be precise, we should talk of emphasis as well as expansion. The object relations theory that has always been inherent in mainstream theory (see Chapter 5) is emphasized and elaborated upon. Psychoanalytic therapy is so much more complex today because we set out to alter not only the relationship among the three agencies, but also between the self representation and the object representations.

Some view the object relations factor overenthusiastically as a new theory and have presented it as departure from the mainstream. I do not regard object relations as a new theory that discards conflict theory in favor a dealing with object relations only. Psychoanalysis and psychoanalytic therapy become more profound as we combine analysis of conflict with attention to interaction between self and object representations.

What Is the Therapeutic Differential?

It is useful here to include consideration of Loewald's (1980) concept of the therapeutic differential. In the course of continuing treatment, the patient becomes aware of the difference between experiences with the primary objects and with the analyst. A reluctant shift takes place as the patient relinquishes morbid internalizations and begins to substitute, selectively, aspects of the current situation. Here, much depends on whether the ego is, or has become, flexible enough to alter fixed modes of self and object relations as reality testing dictates.

Is That Not What the "Innovative" Theories Say?

Yes and no. Yes, there are theories that hold that the relationship with the analyst alters the way a person relates to self and others. No, Loewald does not mean it so simplistically. He means that the internalized self representation acquires new identifications out of the analytic experience. These alter not only the self representation, but also the object representations and the manner in which the two interrelate. I shall refer to that interrelatedness as a pattern.

The Transfer of Function

R. Blanck (1986) proposed that, in the course of structuralization, functions that were aspects of the object representations are transferred to the self representation, thereby furthering the separation-individuation process. What is meant here is not simple operations, such as dressing and feeding oneself, but, more broadly, the continuing climate of care that is the function of the maternal object at the beginning of life and throughout the childhood years. That care especially includes self-esteem, the healthy narcissism that derives from being cared for and cared about. Gradually, the functions of care, love, and responsibility for oneself are transferred over the years until adulthood, when a person is capable of caring for herself and parenting another.

How Much Change Can Be Expected?

Freud already knew that nothing is ever lost. A structure that is laid down may be superseded by later alterations and elaborations, but the basic structure remains and may even exert influence. It follows, therefore, that even with alteration, vestiges of

superseded structure continue to exist. They may lie dormant but
it is not out of the question that unpredictable new life experience may revive them.

Freud knew that when he wrote "Analysis Terminable and
Interminable" in 1937. He said that analysis can only deal with
the events in life, past and present, but not with what may occur
in the future. Psychoanalysis may better equip the individual to
deal with future events, but some events challenge the structure
to the degree that further analysis is indicated.

How Is Structure Altered?

The neurotic patient is presumed to be structured. Treatment
consists largely of alteration of the relationship among the elements of structure by interpretation of conflict, by modification
of the superego, and by selective identification that alters internalized object relations. In such cases, structure is changed but
does not need to be built.

What about Structure Building?

Whereas the neurotic patient is structured, the very essence of
the borderline conditions is that the process of structuralization
is incomplete. This is what makes evaluation and treatment
of the borderline conditions more difficult. The degree of
structuralization varies from case to case and has to be evalu-
ated individually.

For high-level borderline patients, the diagnosis is mixed
because there is incompletion of the separation-individuation
process alongside sufficient structure for some neurotic conflict
to exist. We may refer to such patients as borderline with neurotic features or neurotic with borderline features. With the tech-

nical skill derived from developmental theory, such patients may be analyzed (Stone 1954).

To build structure one first considers the life history, its unique impact upon the individual, the degree of structuralization, and the object relations factor. We take into account also the extent to which separation-individuation has proceeded, and we seek opportunities to further that process.

Other ways of looking at this same separation phenomenon is the degree of independence of the self representations from the object representations, and the degree to which functions of the object representations have been transferred to the self representations.

We seek to detect the places in development where structuralization lagged. As we set development back on track, structure building resumes. The patient's normal developmental thrust does the work. In the case of Mr. Baker (described in Chapter 12), structure was built with fusion of the good and bad object representations into a single representation. It will continue to build as the separation process leads to awareness of self and other as two separate, whole, other persons.

5

Psychoanalytic Object Relations Theory

I once mentioned *British object relations theory* to my editor, and she asked, "Is there an American object relations theory?" I replied that there isn't; there is the totality of psychoanalytic theory that contains an object relations theory within it.

Object relations as a feature of mainstream psychoanalysis is not new. It was known to Freud as early as 1905: "In view of the importance of a child's relations to his parents in determining his later choice of a sexual object, it can easily be understood that any disturbance of those relations will produce the gravest effect on his adult sexual life" (p. 228). In discussing narcissism in 1914, he wrote: "Here we may even venture to touch on the question of what makes it necessary at all for our mental life to pass beyond the limits of narcissism and to attach the libido to objects. . . . We must begin to love if we are not to fall ill, and we are bound to fall ill if, in consequence of frustration, we are unable to love" (p. 85). Freud described anaclitic love as the child's love for the woman who feeds him, the man who protects him, and the succession of substitutes who take their place.

In *Mourning and Melancholia* (1917), Freud linked depression with object loss. In 1921 he commented on the mutual relationship between the ego and the object. By 1923 he wrote as though he took it for granted that object relations is an integral part of psychoanalytic theory: "We cannot avoid giving our attention a moment longer to the ego's object identifications" (p. 30).

Later, as I have noted, the idea of object identifications was expanded to become part of the representational world, the "place" where identifications reside. The very term *identification* implies that there is another person in the picture.

The Expansion of Conflict Theory

With the inclusion of the object relations dimension, psychoanalytic theory became a theory not only of intersystemic conflict (between two of the three agencies of structure) but also of intrasystemic conflict (between the self and object representations).

What Is or Are Object Relations?

This question already states that it is a grammatical nightmare. Is it singular or plural? Said to be an ego function, it is singular. It is an awkward term in other ways as well. The most efficient way of defining it is that it consists of the established pattern of relatedness between the self and object representations. Another way of putting this is to refer to the interaction between the two sets of representations. This establishes object relations as an activity that takes place internally.

The term *object relations* is so embedded in the literature and in communication among analysts that we cannot change it, despite its awkwardness. But there is an alteration that can be made. We are better served to refer not simply to object relations, but to self and object relations because, in the representational world, there are always the two interacting sets of representations.

Why Not Object Relation*ship*?

Object relationship is the interpersonal application of the internalized object relations pattern. It is operational in the sense that the internal aspects or patterning dictate the manner in which a relationship is carried on in the external world.

How Is an Object Relations Pattern Established?

The pattern is created out of the daily affective experiences of the infant and developing child, at first with the mothering person and later with others as well. The child creates this new entity—the pattern—by employing inborn capacities, including ego functions such as cognition and memory, along with affect, to join with the mothering person in forming a relationship. The attuned mother lends herself to the changing needs of the infant and child as they interact almost minute by minute. The affective tone creates an image of the object and of the self. With development, the at-first merged fleeting images become more and more separate and more and more stable.

The relationship, at the outset, is interpersonal. It becomes intrapsychic as internalization fosters formation of images of the self and of the object that arise out of affective experience, later to become, not fleeting images, but stable representations. The intrapsychic transactions and negotiations between the self and object representations fall into patterns that are unique in each individual. We bring our unique pattern of object relations into play in each encounter with another person. As I shall show in Chapter 6, it matters greatly whether the pattern is rigidly fixed or whether there is enough flexibility to allow alteration in the light of the differences between other persons and the primary objects with whom these patterns were originally formed.

What Is the Utility of This Theory?

The pattern of object relations as it operates in a relationship is a way that we "remember" preverbal life. These "memories" remain alive via the manner in which the individual deals with another person. They direct the attitude and behavior toward self and others unconsciously. It is invaluable, in the treatment situation, to assess this behavior in order to gain a picture of the self and object relations pattern and thereby also to gain some inkling of how that pattern arose. These "memories" enable the therapist to reconstruct, speculatively, what might have happened in preverbal life.

How Does This Help Treatment?

The patient brings his or her established pattern of self and object relations into the relationship with the analyst or therapist. In the treatment situation, we call the employment of these patterns *transference*. The manner of behavior toward the analyst, then, provides a replay of early experience. This does not mean that it can be corrected by providing a better experience, as some would conclude logically but simplistically. It means only that we know better what we are dealing with. Some early trauma cannot be corrected, but the patient can be helped to find an adaptation.

Mr. Baker, in psychoanalytic treatment because of a disabling phobia, suffered when the analyst left on vacation or even on ordinary weekends. While so many patients have separation anxiety, this was extreme. It led the analyst to speculate about preverbal life—to think that his mother might have been absent at a critical developmental time. The therapist told the patient tentatively that it was possible that his mother had been away when he was an infant. By asking an older sibling, the patient learned that their mother had gone on an extended trip, lasting about three months, when Mr. Baker was five months old.

Using the observational studies, we know that this is the time when an infant is approaching the second organizer of the psyche—that is, attaining cathexis of the *libidinal object proper* (Spitz). It coincides also with the time when the infant is in the process of *differentiation*—that is, entering the first of the four subphases of the separation-individuation process (Mahler). It is unfortunate that, just as the infant began the long separation-individuation process, his mother left. A child does not know that his mother will return, nor even that she exists in her absence.

In object relations terms, building of self and object images that would normally lead to attainment of the second organizer of the psyche was abruptly disrupted. It is not always possible to repair early trauma. In this case the mother did return. Presumably, there was some resumption of rebuilding of self and object images. But a child whose mother has left rejects her upon her return and then resumes the interaction. This does not mean that the damage is repaired. Later in life, this was reflected in the way that Mr. Baker avoided a close relationship. His behavior upon a first encounter was a barely noticeable negatively tinged distancing. It interfered with his ability to sustain a marriage because he rebuffed his wife's emotional approaches.

During treatment, he telephoned the analyst almost
daily on weekends and vacations. With long-term treatment
he did begin to believe that the analyst existed in his
absence.

Flexibility of the Pattern

The pattern may be rigidly fixed or flexibly alterable. This depends on the competence of ego development and especially the
ego function of reality testing. The more competent ego, capable
of reality testing, can alter the object relations approach to another person in conformity with the reality of the way that other
person is. At best we do not alter our pattern altogether. It remains as an aspect of character.

The less competent the ego, the less capable it is of reality
testing and therefore of altering in accordance with how the other
person really is. Let us use the analogy of the high school physics demonstration. A magnet is placed on a table where there are
scattered iron filings. The filings will be attracted to the magnet. It would require a more powerful magnet to pull them in
another direction. That more powerful magnet is the reality of
the other person pulling an individual away from his or her otherwise automatic tendency to employ the established pattern.

Is There a Self at Birth?

This is controversial. According to psychoanalytic developmental theory the self, or rather the self representation, is born three
years after physical birth (Mahler et al. 1975). Others argue that
there is a self at birth. This matters greatly. If there is a self at
birth, there is little room for development. The major thrust of a
developmental point of view is that development proceeds at an

accelerated pace in early life and at a somewhat slower pace throughout life. In the early months and years development progresses toward acquisition of identity at approximately 3 years of age.

Those who argue that there is a self at birth follow a different theory that is not developmental (Stern 1985). Stern professes to present experimental proof of his position. L. Kaplan (1987) has shown that his experimental design is flawed.

What Is the Role of Object Relations in Treatment?

Object relations patterning determines the manner in which the patient approaches the analyst. One of the major matters to ascertain is whether the patient experiences the analyst or therapist as a separate, whole, other person. If not, to what degree is separation of self representations from object representations operative?

As therapists we train ourselves to be finely tuned instruments as well as receivers. As instruments, we are constantly measuring the degree of structuralization, the level of object relations, as well as the more classical defensive response to conflict and anxiety. As receivers, we listen and record these matters in our minds. As we gain skill, the patterning of object relations will begin to appear as an obvious pathway to ascertaining that most human of all arrangements—what does the individual mean to himself and what do other persons mean to him or her. Yes, I am talking about the capacity to love.

6

Transference

Freud divided pathology into two main groups—the analyzable transference neuroses and the unanalyzable narcissistic neuroses. This was prescient. Although he did not have developmental theory available to him, he came close to present-day division of the pathologies of ambulatory patients into neurotic and borderline—or, in structural terms, structured and understructured. It is the nature of the structure that dictates how the analyst or therapist will deal with the transference, because the structure determines what kind of transference is elaborated.

What Is the Definition of Transference?

There are several definitions of transference. The most generally accepted is that transference is a repetition in the treatment situation of feelings, attitudes, and behavior originally felt toward a primary object, now projected and displaced onto the analyst. Fenichel (1931) was more parsimonious. He defined transference as mistaking the present for the past. This is useful here because the ability to make that distinction is assumed to be present in structured patients and deficient in understructured patients. Another way of putting it is that reality testing, an ego function, is intact in the structured patient and lacking in some degree in the understructured.

I define transference in developmental terms as the deployment of patterned relationships between self and object representations. Since these patterns always exist in each individual, they are used in all other relationships as well as in the transference. Many authors have described transference as ubiquitous.

By this definition, projection and displacement are no longer the most prominent features of transference. What is important now is degree of structuralization, pattern of object relations, and capacity for reality testing.

What Is Projection?

By projection, the person experiences that which is internal as though it emanates from the outside. Jacobson suggested modification of the definition of projection by raising the question of whether, in infants and understructured adults, there can be such a sharp distinction between inside and outside. She reasons that before there is a solid boundary between self and other one cannot project onto another. It is such considerations that force us to redefine transference in developmental terms.

What Is Displacement?

Displacement is a mechanism of defense. As it relates to transference it means that affects and attitudes experienced toward primary objects are now experienced toward the analyst. This speaks of the existence of a cluster of feelings, attitudes, and behavior that belong in the past. It is such a cluster that I believe forms a pattern. If we were to use computer language, we might call it a program because it runs off automatically.

Displacement, then, uses established patterns in dealing with another person that may not be pertinent to the present situation. That suggests that where there is a flaw in, or temporary suspension of, reality testing, the individual not only mistakes the present for the past, but deals with present-day objects according to the established patterns, disregarding how they really are.

What about Regression?

Regression plays an important role in transference. Under the stress of need, the patient regresses. Those with a competent enough ego regress "in the service of the ego." They are able to recover from the regression when it is appropriate to do so, such as returning to the real world after an analytic session.

In understructured patients regression is a more serious matter and needs to be controlled wherever possible. These patients are already at a less developed level and usually need to progress rather than regress. Always to be borne in mind as well is that recoverability from regression is not reliable in such cases.

What Is the Role of Structure in Transference?

Degree of structuralization influences whether the object relations pattern, used in dealing with the therapist or analyst, is rigidly fixed or flexibly alterable in the light of reality. Structuralization also determines whether a transference is interpretable or uninterpretable. The transference of the structured patient is interpretable, given the correct timing; that of the understructured patient is uninterpretable.

The structured patient, having a competent ego, uses the function of reality testing most of the time. She is able, except when in the throes of the transference, to know that, although the analyst may appear to be *like* her father, he is not really her father. A timely interpretation informs the patient of the confusion of past with present, and because reality testing is intact, she is then able to use the interpretation to make the distinction.

The understructured patient, on the other hand, engages in a relationship with the therapist that, strictly speaking, is not truly a transfer from past to present. Precision would demand that we not call it transference, but we are unable to alter that because the term remains in common usage. For precision and fine tuning, I find it useful to distinguish between transference from past to present, on the one hand, and perpetuation of early patterns of self and object relations, on the other.

The understructured patient is suffering from perpetuation of the failure to have developed a separate self representation. The therapist is, in some degree, experienced as part of the self representation because the object representations are incompletely sorted out from the representation of the self, a developmental task that normally is carried out in the process of attaining psychological birth. Pointing out the difference between past and present—that is, interpreting the transference—is ineffective in those kinds of structures. The past dominates the present. It is for that reason that I regard the transference of the understructured patient as uninterpretable.

What Is the Role of Anxiety?

It is usually anxiety that causes the structured patient to suspend reality testing temporarily. But, in such patients, that function is never altogether lost. The understructured patient, less able to tolerate anxiety, clings more tenaciously to familiar self and object representations. Whatever degree of reality testing has been attained is colored by the effort to retain tenuous connection with the object representations. To attempt to interpret under such circumstances may force such a patient to an even more desperate attempt at retention of the incompletely separated object representations, thus defeating the interpretation. If the patient does not retain the still merged self and object representations, there is object loss and loss of self, a serious decompensation.

What to Do, Then?

In dealing with the transference of the structured patient it may even be desirable to allow the "mistake" to continue for a while so that the patient may experience the full force of it. This may be done safely in such cases. It is not safe to do that with an understructured patient, for that would only perpetuate the unreality without leading the patient into the real world.

The understructured patient is not mistaking the present for the past so much as living in the past. Therefore, she cannot process an interpretation that points out a mistake she does not feel she is making. The therapist is in somewhat of a dilemma here because it is not advisable to allow perpetuation of the past, and yet it is also contraindicated to try to deprive the patient of the object representations to which she clings. The safest and most productive course is to build structure to the point where interpretation becomes possible—to build the ego toward capability of distinguishing past from present. We build structure by helping the patient establish more solid boundaries. This follows from Mahler's definition of the borderline patient as having failed to complete the separation-individuation process.

Clinical Illustration

An understructured man in his thirties says that he feels like a baby. He is tall, well built, and looks altogether like a man. The therapist is a relatively small woman. The patient says, "I am a baby and I want to sit in your lap." This disregards reality even to the point of failing to see that it would be physically impossible. The therapist says, "If you were a baby, I would hold you."

What Does That Do?

First, to what it does not do. It does not interpret that he behaves with the therapist as though she is his mother. It does not even inform him that the therapist is not his mother. At his level of structuralization such interpretations would be meaningless.

The intervention, not interpretation, that was made deals with his impaired reality testing while not deriding his wish. By putting it in the subjunctive, the therapist removes it from the realm of possibility while at the same time validating that it is an appropriate wish for a baby to have. Putting it this way also orients him in time; he is no longer a baby, although he still has baby needs.

One Person or Two?

Transference—the deployment of the object relations pattern in the treatment situation—is the indispensable context within which treatment is carried out. Understanding its import supports the position that the therapist and analyst provide a clear field for this phenomenon to play itself out without contamination by the countertransference.

How Is the Countertransference Used?

Countertransference has acquired a negative connotation, as though it should not exist in ideal situations. That, of course, is absurd. I have stressed that there are two persons in a therapy session. The therapist or analyst is a person with thoughts, fantasies, and affects. Every patient has impact. The technical issue here is how to deal with that impact. If we have a strong reaction to a patient, our first obligation is to examine ourselves. Does this reaction arise from our own issues that have nothing to do with the patient, or is the patient instilling it? That makes a huge difference. If we are having a personal reaction, we analyze it without involving the patient. If it is so severe that we cannot analyze it alone, we seek help from another analyst or supervisor.

The most useful aspect of countertransference is understanding what the patient is instilling. Is the patient being seductive, trying to elicit anger, putting us to sleep? These responses are not necessarily interpreted on the spot. We use them to understand the patient and work them into the ongoing process, interpreting them as parts of the larger issues.

A seductive patient, for example, is using an object relations approach that repeats the relationship with a parent. That gives the analyst the flavor of what the early situation was like. It can be used to help the patient understand that she carries this object relations pattern over into situations that are not always appropriate in the present.

Some patients try to provoke an angry response. Once again, that tells us something about the object relations pattern. Of course, we do not play in with that, nor is it useful to make the simplistic interpretation, "You are trying to make me angry." Instead, one considers that this may be a defense against closeness, or a way of instigating a reaction that was needed to get a parent to react, or any number of similar reasons.

Some patients try to lull us to sleep. They drone on and we get sleepy. First it is necessary to examine whether we really are sleepy. A patient behaved this way midmorning, when the analyst was usually fresh and alert. The analyst thought about why he felt sleepy and realized that the patient was lulling him. He pondered why the patient needed to do this. A good hypothesis was that the patient feared the analyst's affects and felt more comfortable if they were toned down. This helped the analyst understand something about the patient, which is the ideal way to use the countertransference. There is usually no need to convey this to the patient immediately. Interpretation always awaits the proper timing.

I have tried to convey a position about countertransference with which not all analysts agree these days. Some advocate using the countertransference to demonstrate to the patient how he is behaving. I do not go along with that because I believe that to confront a person with his behavior does not go far enough and can be pejorative, as though we know better how a person is to behave. It may appear critical, judgmental, or negative in other ways. It has little or no mutative effect. It may, in some instances, get the patient to alter his behavior. But then we are getting into a different modality. In psychoanalytic therapy, alteration of behavior comes about through insight into why one behaves in a certain way—defensively, or following an object relations pattern. The psychoanalytic therapeutic objective of understanding defenses and of altering the object relations pattern is more profound, I believe, than altering behavior.

The use of the transference and countertransference, then, follows the theoretical theme that the major objectives of psychoanalytic therapy are to alter structure, to build structure where it is lacking, to alter basic object relations patterns, and to deal with defenses and the conflicts that lie beneath them.

7

Descriptive Developmental Diagnosis

This chapter discusses psychoanalytic developmental diagnosis, which is different from diagnosis based on the *Diagnostic and Statistical Manual of Mental Disorders* (*DSM-IV*) (American Psychiatric Association 1994). Developmental diagnosis takes symptoms into account, as does *DSM-IV*, but does not rely on them because the same symptoms can exist in different structures.

For a long time I thought I was stating the obvious when I said that diagnosis is needed in order to know where to address treatment. Yet, in supervising analysts and therapists, I found such eagerness to get the treatment going that some tended to begin before knowing more than the presenting problem.

Psychoanalytic developmental diagnosis involves ascertaining the patient's structure, level of self and object relations, defences, conflicts, and developmental lesions. My emphasis is on evaluating the structure to know whether to analyze conflict in the neurotic structure, or to build structure in the borderline patient. Other terms for this process are *assessment* and *evaluation*. I prefer *diagnosis* because I believe it is more precise.

Don't the Symptoms Tell the Diagnosis?

Unreliably. The degree of separation and level of structuralization is not as easily ascertained as are symptoms. Although in medicine symptoms are a more certain guide to diagnosis, even there it is not always so. As is well known, a headache is a symptom of many illnesses ranging from tension to brain tumor. In psychopathology, matters are even more complex. An example is obsessive-compulsive symptomatology. It can be indicative of compromise formation in neurosis, it can be a defense against full-blown psychosis, it can be a borderline phenomenon, or, if not too extreme, it can fall within the normal range of orderliness.

How Can Symptoms Mislead?

We might encounter two patients who present at a given developmental level. One patient is suffering from a developmental arrest at that level. The other has reached a higher developmental level and, to defend against anxiety, has regressed to the lower level. Although they appear the same, the treatment plan is very different for each. The patient who is fixated is probably understructured and needs help in the direction of developing beyond that point. The patient who has regressed is probably structured and uses regression as a defense. A structured patient would be infantalized if treated at the regressed level.

Relax, the Patient Will Return

One reason therapists sometimes give for beginning treatment quickly is to establish rapport or to give the patient a taste of treatment so that he will return. With experience, a therapist learns that those devices for holding the patient are not necessary. The problem itself will motivate the patient to return.

Developmental Diagnosis

I have said that the type of diagnosis I am speaking about is not a one-time thing, although it is crucial to know at the outset whether the patient is an analyzable (structured) neurotic or a borderline (understructured) personality. Knowing at least that much guides the therapist toward establishing an appropriate treatment plan.

A neurotic patient is to be analyzed on a schedule of at least four times per week. Some types of borderline patients are unable to tolerate such frequency and closeness. Such patients are seen two or three times per week. Once-a-week treatment has become popular, not for diagnostic reasons, but for expediency. I do not favor once-a-week therapy except for patients who are very disturbed (low-level borderline), cannot develop further, and need to be maintained at the level where they are, lest they regress even further.

Is Diagnosis Once and Forever?

Diagnosis goes on throughout the treatment. It can even alter the direction of treatment as new information is added. In the sense in which I am speaking, diagnosis goes hand in hand with treatment. It has even been said that we do not know the precise diagnosis until the case is at an end. This seeming paradox is explained by the fact that we cannot get to know everything about the patient at once, and that new material emerges throughout treatment. A complexity is added by the very definition of treat-

ment—to alter the diagnosis for the better. With competent treatment, therefore, the diagnosis should keep changing.

What Is Developmental Diagnosis?

First I shall talk about what it is not. It does not resemble the
DSM type of diagnosis. The *DSM* was designed for statistical
purposes, to enter a code number on a chart or insurance form.
It does not tell anything about the development of the individual, only about the symptoms, and it offers no guide to
treatment.

Developmental diagnosis, on the other hand, looks verti-
cally at the patient's life history and fits together how she has
developed over the years and how the ego has adapted to the events
in her life. Of special concern is the level of structuralization that
the patient has reached or to which she has regressed. We also
look at the nature of the conflicts, the appropriateness of the
affects, and the level of self and object relations. It is also of
great importance to consider whether the patient experiences
us as a separate, whole, other person, for that is a measure of
the completion of the separation-individuation process.

What Do You Mean by Separation?

I certainly do not mean physical separation for, especially in
infancy, the person is not equipped to live a separate life. Separation involves the gradual sorting out of images of a self, at first
merged with images of the mothering person, until a separate
identity is established. That is why Mahler refers to it as a process. By the time of psychological birth at approximately 3 years
of age, the child has separate images of self and other that

stabilize as representations. In concert with that development, structuralization and internalization have also proceeded.

What Shall We Look For?

I will present a guide to ascertaining the level of development and structuralization. In a given case, it is not necessary to answer every criterion raised in this guide. With experience, one learns to use it selectively, ferreting out two or three developmental issues that help the therapist know how to begin the treatment. These criteria are kept in mind by the therapist and, as they are answered, become hypotheses only. As the treatment progresses and more information is obtained, the hypothesis may alter many times.

Developmental Criteria

> The drives are channeled by a competent ego. This means that the ego has developed from birth, through the developmental phases, to the point where it is strong enough to be in control of the drives.
> Thought is used as trial action. The drives are thereby subjected to the ego functions of judgment and delay of action, and may be channeled in directions that function adaptively for the individual.
> The ego has the capacity to tolerate frustration, conflict, and anxiety.
> There is capacity for self observation.
> The ego has the capacity for organization and, when new elements are added, for reorganization.
> The representational world is established.

The level of object relations is triadic more than dyadic.
The oedipal level has been approached.

Is the Oedipal Conflict a Pathology?

Freud designated the oedipal conflict as the core conflict in
neurosis. Although a neurosis is a pathology, it represents a
high level of development and, as stated, is indicative of structuralization and of a strong ego capable of tolerating conflict and
anxiety.

In the normal course of development, the child who successfully negotiates the *separation-individuation process* to attain psychological birth also reaches the oedipal level. This suggests that the oedipal conflict is a normal developmental stage.
The question arises because, in neurosis, as Freud said, the conflict is not resolved.

Can the Oedipal Conflict Be Resolved?

We think now that resolution goes through many rounds. In
fortunate circumstances, it is sufficiently resolved in the first
round to enable the child to enter latency. It reemerges in adolescence, where it has to undergo another round of resolution
(Blos 1962). We (Blanck and Blanck 1968) have suggested that
marriage is still another round in what is probably a lifetime
process.

Is Every Patient's Development Stalled?

Development never comes to a full halt. Aspects of development
may be impaired, but the onward thrust of development proceeds

nevertheless, incorporating the flaw. In some fortunate instances the flaw may even be overcome. Mahler thought that an adequate rapprochement subphase can correct some of the inadequacies of the earlier subphases. Yet, as we saw in the case of Mr. Baker, an early trauma could not be repaired. This does not prove Mahler wrong. Mr. Baker might have had a less-than-adequate rapprochement as well.

What Can You Tell from the Transference?

Transference is sometimes formed even before the patient sees us. At the contemplation of making the telephone call, images from the past in the form of how the therapist is wished to be are already in the process of formation. At the first telephone call these may be reinforced or altered. That illustrates why the transference has been called ubiquitous—the operation of the object relations pattern that the individual applies to everyone.

As the contact with the therapist increases, the special arrangement of the therapeutic situation brings about a transference that is more specific. The therapist begins to resemble one or both parents. That is because of the controlled regression in the treatment, especially of neurotic structures. Therapy is deliberately arranged as a situation of inequality—one person is in need of help and the other is seen as *in loco parentis.* That is a politically incorrect stance in our society. But politics and sociological fashions have no place in science.

Usually a patient is well into treatment before transferential features become usable. Nevertheless, in the very first session, even sometimes in the first phone call, close examination of the manner in which the patient deals with us tells much, especially about the level of self and object relations.

How Do You Go About Diagnosing, Then?

We discover our own methods as we accumulate experience in diagnosis. My method is to allow the patient a certain amount of unstructured time so that she can tell her story in her own way. I listen for clues about development, structuralization, the nature of the conflict, whether the affect is consonant with what the patient is saying, and whether I am being dealt with as a separate, whole, other person, or in some degree as part of the self representations.

After a while, I begin to structure the session more by asking questions that have been raised in my mind as the patient was talking. I seek fulfillment of the criteria stated above with the expectation that not all diagnostic issues will be answered.

8

Beginning the Treatment

This chapter discusses the challenges that the psychotherapist encounters in beginning a case. Psychoanalysts face such problems to a lesser extent because a patient who consents to analysis has overcome the initial hurdle of ambivalence about being there. I do not mean that the ambivalence ceases to exist, and certainly we expect resistance as part of the process. I mean merely that the beginning is different.

To begin the treatment, one must be aware of the obstacles and limitations, both within the patient and from outside sources. Especially these days, outside limitations impose requirements upon the therapist that impair the decisions that, ideally, are to be made by therapist and patient only. Those limitations have always come from clinic policies and supervisors. The most cumbersome limitations now are imposed by third party payers.

Limitations on the patient's side stem from ambivalence. (Resistance is another matter, which I shall deal with separately.) It is hardly possible for a person to present herself for treatment wholeheartedly. The degree of ambivalence varies from one person to another. The therapist must know how to use it to give the case a positive turn.

The Prospective Patient

Many prospective psychotherapy patients who appear in the consultation room are not yet truly patients. They come for a variety of reasons, sometimes because they want to be treated, but often with much ambivalence. Usually the therapist, aware of the person's reservations, can proceed nevertheless when the negative side of the ambivalence is outweighed by the urgency of the problem. The person who consciously wants help can begin. The negative side will become therapeutic material later.

The Reluctant Prospect

The reluctant patient is sometimes referred to as difficult. But I do not believe that there are difficult patients; there is only our difficulty in understanding them. Some patients say openly, "I did not want to come." This is because the person, not yet a patient, has been sent by a spouse, clergyman, teacher, or employer. The obvious response, "So why are you here?" will propel the person out the door. Emphasis is placed upon the fact that the person is present. She did not act on not wanting to come; she came. In such a situation the opportunity may exist only once. It is to be seized.

Limitations Because of Anxiety

Some prospective patients announce limitations at the outset. "I only want a little help." We cultivate a particular way of listening. Delete *only* and *a little*. What is left is, "I want help." Anxiety has caused the person to say, in effect, "Don't go too fast." The therapist responds, "We will do as much as you want." This puts control back into the patient's hands so that she can proceed at a pace that is comfortable for her.

The Hazards of Leaping Too Quickly

Because a person has made an appointment and kept it, it is all too easy for the therapist to fall into the trap of beginning treatment with someone who is not yet motivated. This happens all too often because of therapeutic zeal. The therapist plunges ahead, leaving the patient's indecision far behind. If treatment is begun without the person's consent and participation, resentment and anger will build. The case may terminate abruptly.

What to Do, Then?

Do not need the patient. This may seem odd at first glance. It means only that need conveyed to a negative person will cause him to want to deprive you. This does not mean that we do not show interest, but as I shall illustrate in some dialogue, it has to be interest in how the person feels. We can be relatively certain that the person who comes wants help, no matter how negatively she presents herself.

The short answer to the question about what to do is: capture the affect.

The "Sent" Prospect

The greatest challenge is presented by a person who was sent. A man comes because his wife says that he is not a good-enough father to their children. He says he has come for advice on how to do better. The therapist notes two things to herself: (1) He does not "own" the problem. (2) He presents himself as compliant. We ask ourselves: Has he come in obedience to his wife, or in defiance? In order to tell her that he has been there? Is there a place where the problem bothers him? Can the therapist touch it?

What Not to Do

Do not accept the presenting complaint at face value. It would be a poor beginning to agree with his wife that he is not a good father and try to make him better. Ask what he thinks. "As long as you are here, let us talk about it," may slant the emphasis away from how bad he is. While listening to his story, one looks for where something might be troubling him.

> *Prospective patient:* I came because my wife nagged me so much I decided to get her off my back.
>
> *Therapist:* That's a heavy load, having your wife on your back.
>
> *PP:* I never thought of it that way, but you are right. Anyway, now I can tell her I've done it.
>
> *Therapist:* Will that end the problem for you? (Turns to the person's feelings, taking focus off the wife's viewpoint.)
>
> *PP:* No, she'll be at me again.
>
> *Therapist:* Why does she do that?
>
> *PP:* Well, I don't always please her.
>
> *Therapist:* That must be unpleasant for you.
>
> *PP:* I feel I am not so bad. I do lots of things with the kids. (He realizes the therapist is not going to look for flaws in him.)
>
> *Therapist:* (Takes advantage of his reference to his feelings.) I think you do not feel good enough about yourself.
>
> *PP:* Well, I do want to please her, but I can never do enough.

Therapist: So it was hard for you to come here because you believe that I, too, will fault you.

PP: Isn't that what this is all about?

Therapist: It is about trying to help you with a troubling situation. Obviously you want to get along with your wife. I get the sense that life would be better for you if you did not feel so criticized. (Takes the focus away from where he feels at fault.)

PP: That would be a relief.

Therapist: If you like, we can try to work in that direction.

PP: I'll give it a try.

What Has Happened?

A prospective patient has become a patient. How? The therapist was not misled into accepting the wife's view of the problem. The matter had to be redirected—from the way the wife feels to the way he feels. Concern for his feelings turned the tide.

As treatment progresses it may be that he does feel that he is not a good-enough father. He does not want to be criticized for it and will only acknowledge it when he feels that the therapist is there to help him with his feelings about being a father. He will become interested in exploration. We may, for example, find that he lacks a solid internalized representation of himself as he interacted with his own father.

Laypersons refer to this as lacking a "role model." That is too thin. To model oneself after another person is copying without internalizing. Even if we use the term *identification* it does not hold true that one can only be the way one's parent was. Identification is always partial or, as Jacobson put it, selective. We

combine selected traits of our parents, but create out of it something from ourselves.

     In the case under discussion, then, we have to get the pa-
tient past blaming his own father and deal with his feelings about
himself in that role, how he feels about his children. When he
knows that blame is not in the picture, the case will proceed.

The Therapist's Anxiety

Therapists do become anxious, especially when working to
secure the case while the patient is being challenging. Robert
Knight pioneered in the treatment of the borderline conditions in
the 1950s when little was known about them. He described how
puzzled he was as he passed an open door to the treatment room
in a hospital where he was teaching. He saw two anxious persons
and asked himself who is the patient and who is the therapist. Then
he noted that the person in the white coat must be the therapist.

Outside Limitations

Third-party payers intrude on professional decisions. Before that
vexing situation came about, therapists have lived with other
limitations. There are always the extraneous ones such as the
patient living at a distance, jobs that do not allow the patient time
for therapy, financial considerations, and clinic rules.

Supervision

The only valid intrusion upon a case is supervision. Essential as
it is for training purposes, it can impair the conduct of the case
and the transference. I do not favor telling the patient that her
case is under supervision. Often patients who come through low-

cost arrangements are told that. Although we know of no other way that a therapist can be trained, knowledge of someone looking over the therapist's shoulder burdens both patient and therapist. The therapist needs to be aware of this phenomenon and try to minimize it.

Other Limitations

We are faced with more subtle limitations within the patient. Many patients externalize—project to the outside. "My boss gets me upset." "My mother nags me." The problem lies outside because it has become ego syntonic.

What Does Ego Syntonic Mean?

Persons who feel that the problem lies outside themselves are at dearly bought peace. The ego accepts that one's feelings and behavior are natural and justified by the circumstances. This comes very close to and even coincides with avoidance of narcissistic injury. It is a thick wall that protects against hurt. We help such patients best when we realize that underneath the bravado lies great vulnerability. In dealing with that it is of the utmost importance to present a neutral nonjudgmental stance. We do that with all patients, of course, but here it is the very attitude that will turn the tide. Slowly the patient becomes more comfortable, less on guard, and more willing to endure discomfort in a benign climate.

The Benign Climate

This refers to the atmosphere that the therapist creates within which the patient is made to feel welcome, comfortable, unjudged, and empathized with. We keep our appointments on time. We avoid interruptions such as phone calls. For most if not all patients, the very reliability of the therapist is a new experience. Hardly any other situation exists that is devoted entirely to the sole benefit of the person in need of help.

How to Design the Treatment

I have described how to help the prospective patient become a patient in her own right, to "own" the problem, to be willing to be treated for it. In the public mind, therapy has become a once-a-week matter. For most problems, that limitation is undesirable. Ideally, the therapist decides on the frequency of the treatment based on the diagnosis. Often one has to go along with whatever the patient can tolerate in the beginning, with the expectation that as he gets more deeply into the process the proper frequency will be worked out between patient and therapist.

Therapeutic Alliance

The man who feared that he is not a good father was brought into a therapeutic alliance by the therapist who found that he would join in exploring his feelings. There are several definitions of therapeutic alliance. The one I like refers to therapeutic seizure of the wish to get well and turning that into a mutual goal. As we encourage that part of the ego to join in the endeavor, we remain aware that there is also a part that will work against that objective. It helps to bear in mind that the so-called resistance is never against the therapist, but to defend against anxiety.

Resistance

Resistance is one of several words borrowed from the common vocabulary and given a different meaning in psychoanalytic technique. Since we learn it in its common meaning first, we are prone to get caught up in that. Patients who are aware of some reluctance will call themselves resistant as though they are scolding themselves before the therapist will scold them. This, of course, is mistaken. By definition, resistance is unconscious. It is defined as the use of defense in the therapeutic situation. A patient without resistance is seriously understructured. Seen in that light, resistance is to be welcomed. In structural terms, the ego employs defenses against anxiety. Never is resistance against the therapist or the therapy.

Beginning a case is difficult because that is when we know the least about the patient. Yet a certain ease can be obtained if the diagnostic phase includes inquiry that helps the therapist feel secure in what he is doing. Often attention to the affective state can shift the prospective patient into becoming a patient, as illustrated in the dialogue with the prospective patient cited above.

9

A Model Case

I present a model case to illustrate the theory, the diagnosis, and the recommendations for treatment. I describe the case first as it would be diagnosed and treated without restriction. In Chapter 11 I discuss how to best serve the patient when extraneous factors limit the therapy.

The Case

Mr. Abel is a 35-year-old man who came with the presenting problem of trouble on the job. His coworkers teased and taunted him because he was still living at his parents' home and not dating. It would have stopped after a while if they had not sensed his vulnerability. But when they saw how seriously he took what they thought of as a joke, they kept at it. They called him names—sissy, momma's boy—and said maybe he was gay. It so upset him that his job performance began to suffer. He could not go to the water cooler or men's room for fear of encountering someone who would taunt him. The employer's health plan referred him for "counseling."

History

The history was elicited gradually in the course of the diagnosis and treatment and is presented here in summarized form.

Mr Abel is the youngest of three boys. The parents were not happy about having another boy, although they would have welcomed a girl. As a baby, the patient got what laypersons call "lots of attention." This means that he was everyone's plaything—a teddy bear for his brothers, and company for his mother when his father was at work and the older boys were at school.

That he was played with as a toy for their pleasure did not offer the same developmental opportunity as would have been the case if they had played when he needed it and at his level. But no one in the family was interested in playing for the purpose of furthering his development. They had their own needs. The brothers enjoyed rolling him on the floor; his mother enjoyed cuddling; his father was indifferent. None of these was necessarily what he needed or when he needed it. These appear to be small matters, but they are examples of how a child can grow up in a less-than-optimal developmental climate. The damage is subtle and tends not to be noticed. "Lots of attention" hardly ever coincided with his changing developmental needs. The cuddling came when his lonely mother needed it. The roughhousing by his brothers frightened and overstimulated him. He needed his father as well as his brothers for his masculine identification.

One of the major roles of the father in a child's early life is to lure him or her out of the close tie to the mother. The maternal tie is necessary, but becomes too much of a good thing if prolonged in a way that obstructs progress to the next developmental level. Later, for both boy and girl, paternal interest is necessary.

Yet Mr. Abel's development was not altogether halted. We have to credit his innate endowment that enabled him to extract developmental supplies. Also, although the attention was not optimal, he was not unattended. To put this another way, he did not lack objects who could be internalized to become part of his object world.

Why Was Development Inadequate, Then?

His developmental needs were not met at the phase-appropriate time. That skews development in some respects. The child has an inadequate partner in the developmental endeavor, leaving him to rely to a large extent on his own abilities. A well-endowed child can make this adaptation. But the result for Mr. Abel was an object relations pattern containing an attitude toward self and other that prevents him from seeking appropriate fulfillment of need in smoother interaction with others.

Stranger Anxiety

When he was 9 months old the parents went on a cruise. An aunt offered to take the children into her home while the parents were away. The older boys suffered their parents' absence and living in a place that was not home. The baby suffered even more. He was at the developmental stage when he had begun to distinguish familiar faces from the faces of strangers. That was when the familiar ones left.

Wasn't the Aunt Familiar?

Yes, he had seen her before. But at about 9 months, the child begins to recognize mother as a very special person and becomes leery of strangers. When she returned, he turned away from her. To all appearances, that lasted only a day or two and all seemed well again. But these events leave scars that influence how a person feels about himself in relation to others. The patient was imperceptively saddened and less trusting. Those feelings are reawakened when later events tap into them.

The Practicing Subphase

When he began to crawl and then toddle, it was too hard for mother to keep up with him. She had other things to do. It is important for the development of an ambulatory child to have the freedom to explore his world with parental vigilance limited to keeping him out of danger. This patient's mother exercised vigilance, not in the service of his development, but because it was an inconvenience to have to follow him around. She restrained him, impressing upon him early in life that it is dangerous to explore his circumscribed world. This had a lasting effect upon his oedipal development, as we shall see shortly.

Gender Identity

Gender identity was shaky because, although he had his father and brothers with whom to identify, he was with his mother more. Her disappointment that her third child was not a girl was never stated to him, but there is an unconscious communication. Did it make him dissatisfied with himself?

Adaptation

He needed his mother and had to work so hard to keep her with him. When such adaptation persists into adulthood, as it usually does because the self and object relations pattern is established, it becomes maladaptive.

Separation

Gradual separation, not in the physical sense but in slowly acquiring a separate identity, was a struggle for him. It appears as though he made it because of his favorable innate endowment. Although we care less about physical separation, it sometimes reflects the internal situation. He had a hard time going off to school at age 5, which was repeated when he went off to college many years later. In high school he had tried dating, but didn't enjoy it because of his less than firm gender identity and because of repression of his sexual wishes.

In college he found a young woman who also had separation problems, a common freshman malady. They were together constantly throughout college and thought they would marry eventually. Sex was not as important as being together. After graduation, she did not want to live in his hometown because it was too far away from her home. He, too, wanted to be at home, and so he returned alone.

Individuation

Mr. Abel individuated in that he used his endowment to progress in those aspects that did not put him in conflict with need for maternal nurturing. A well-endowed person whose phase-appropriate partnering in early life is deficient can individuate without separating. This is because individuation is less dependent on the attunement or unattunement of the partner.

How Do the Defenses Reveal the Structure?

The ego employs defense when conflict causes anxiety. I have pointed out that Mr. Abel uses competent defense mechanisms. Were he less adequately structured, these would not be available to him because the ego would not be up to the defensive task. A competent ego is an indicator of structuralization.

What Did These Defenses Do for Him?

They enabled him to grapple with his oedipal wishes by repressing them and regressing—beating a quick retreat to the safety of his relationship with his preoedipal mother. The regressive cushion against anxiety was ready-made for him because his mother had been most interested in him as a preoedipal child who remained close to her. His father and brothers were formidable rivals; his fear of his own aggressive wishes was great. Safety required repression of sexual yearnings. The analyst encounters him in the regressed state of attachment to the preoedipal mother.

What Is a Preoedipal Mother?

We have to talk about the same person in two different roles. It is not the mother who changes, but the child's perception of her. Mr. Abel sought the preoedipal mother, not necessarily as she really was, but in fantasy—as a protector against the terror of his oedipal wishes. His mother in real life no longer plays much of a role. His unconscious memory of her as a protector exists because in childhood he needed to think of her in that way, and to some extent she acted in that role. As an adult, then, he uses this to keep him safe from separation, from venturing into an adult life, from oedipal wishes, and from a contemporary sex partner.

Affect

Mr. Abel's affect appears to be appropriate to what he is saying. In another case that might not be so. Again, a less developed person might feel one way and act another. His affect would not be in tune with his behavior. He might laugh when talking about something serious, not nervously as some people do, but because his affect does not match up with what he is talking about.

Anger

Suppression and later repression of anger began in the separation-individuation process when opposition to his mother's restraints was too hard to assert. Thus, Mr. Abel had frustrating, rage-producing experiences long before the oedipal position.

On the positive side, he developed a capacity to love. That became too dangerous at the oedipal level when love is intermingled with sexual desire.

Developmental Diagnostic Statement

Here I present the descriptive developmental diagnosis of Mr. Abel as a guide to treatment. This diagnosis is quite different from the *DSM* diagnosis.

Mr. Abel is neurotic as defined by being structured and having reached the oedipal level. He defends against oedipal strivings by repressing them and regressing to a lower level of development.

Although his development has lagged, his good innate endowment enabled him to extract enough supplies from a less-than-adequate environment so that structuralization could proceed without much help from outside. This is accomplished at a price that will become known in the course of the treatment.

He is structured. We know that because of what he has accomplished in life and, more important than external factors, because he is capable of using high-level defenses such as repression and regression. These are reflections of a competent ego, which is a most important part of structure.

I proposed (Blanck 1984) that an adequate practicing subphase prepares for later venture. Although it provides courage to venture, it does not prepare the child to engage in conflict. That is not a flaw in the subphase, which serves another developmental purpose. Intersystemic conflict can only arise when the structure is established. The practicing subphase child has not yet reached that developmental level.

Conflict

Mr. Abel has both oedipal and preoedipal conflicts. The preoedipal conflicts are between the self and object representations that have not been established smoothly. The growth-promoting thrust of the aggressive drive that would propel separation is in conflict with his residual need for mothering. This also serves to prevent resolution of the oedipal conflict because anxiety about aggressive wishes causes the ego to employ regression. Thus, one conflict fits with the other, leading him to find refuge in the preoedipal mother.

Anxiety

We do not want to cause a patient unnecessary pain. Anxiety becomes tolerable if it arises within the context of a strong transference and at the right time. One reason why I have stressed diagnosis is that the less structured patient, because of a less competent ego, can be overwhelmed by anxiety. If we have di-

agnosed well, we will know that the patient is well-enough structured, has a competent ego, and is using defenses that were perhaps necessary in childhood but have become maladaptive now.
Such a patient can tolerate anxiety in the interest of resolving
his conflict. Resolution of oedipal conflict will enable him to find
a suitable partner, to marry, perhaps to become a father. He will
be able to assert himself when necessary, and in an appropriate
manner.

Curtailed treatment would not achieve all this, but may be
contributory if conducted with the larger picture in the therapist's
mind.

The Full Bucket

I refer to optimal treatment—psychoanalysis—as a full bucket
because this enables me to describe curtailed treatment as drops
in the bucket, useful as far as they go, but not enough to fill the
bucket. Optimal treatment would involve the kind of personality overhaul that is only possible with full-fledged psychoanalysis. I describe what the full treatment would consist of so that
the therapist who has to do something short of that will contribute the right drops. Maybe there will be several bouts of treatment throughout the patient's life. The "right" drops are those
that are based on the same diagnostic evaluation and proceed in
the same treatment direction.

In the next chapter I describe treatment short of psychoanalysis. There may be several bouts of treatment. If each one
adds another correct drop, the advantages will accrue. The wrong
drops will detract.

10

Behind the Scenes
of the Model Case

We begin with Mr. Abel's relationship with his mother, basing this on our theoretical assumption that the first task of a neonate is to fit together with his environment and to adapt to it (Hartmann). Usually, that environment is the mothering person.

We know that Mr. Abel's mother would have preferred a girl. We are permitted to speculate that her disappointment affected him at the outset. This kind of speculation, based on the findings of the child observationalists, is helpful in trying to imagine the climate of the patient's infancy.

What Else May We Speculate?

An infant can sense the mother's affect. Did she hold him less lovingly because of her disappointment, because of maternal shortcomings, because of involvement with other family matters? Did she hasten the weaning? Did she give him a bottle to hold by himself?

What Is Wrong with a Held Bottle?

If a child needs a nursing bottle, he should be held just as when he is breast-feeding. When a child is given the bottle to hold by himself, he establishes a relationship with the bottle, an inanimate object that cannot provide interaction. With a real person, there is opportunity for the kind of give and take that, in a good-enough circumstance, promotes psychological growth. My guess is that Mr. Abel did hold his own bottle and that his mother was thus relieved of the job of holding him.

How Is Such a Hypothesis Justified?

I am guided by the quality of object relations in real life and in the transference. Mr. Abel's attitude toward the other person is reflective of an imbalance of self representation, with too much emphasis on the object representations. Another way of describing this is that his self-esteem is lowered.

It does not matter whether I am correct about the held bottle. If it proves to be incorrect as a historical event, one would still have to note that he turns inward in a narcissistic direction and expects too little of other persons. We see that there were similar attitudes in other, rememberable aspects of development. But we must not think about these affronts as total. If they had been, he would not have developed as well as he did and would have been rendered unable to function on the level on which we now encounter him. Flaws invade development and skew it, but development proceeds nevertheless, carrying the flaws along with it.

How Would He Have Known How His Mother Felt?

Affect is transmitted to the neonate, who has a keen awareness of affective communication. Spitz (1959) designated this as *coenesthetic sensing*, by which he meant that the mode of communication when the neonate has barely emerged from the womb is finely attuned to affects that emanate from the unfamiliar and as yet unknown outside world. This kind of affective, visceral sensing becomes an unrememerable experience that, nevertheless, colors the person's attitude toward himself in relation to his world.

We cannot know with certainty how his mother felt or how that was conveyed to him by the way he was held. It is merely something to think about. You may call that speculation, assumption, or hypothesis. But bear in mind that it is based on careful observation of neonates. Affective sensing forms unrememberable experiences that lend subtle coloring to the person's character.

We have to think, then, about whether and how such very early experience influenced Mr. Abel's way of relating to others. And, taking his mother's general attitude toward him into account, how that works in with his later mother–child experiences. We look for how these cumulative experiences have influenced the pattern of his relationship to self and others.

Where Shall We Look?

The most telling place is the transference. He will demonstrate, in his behavior toward the therapist, how he feels about himself and how he deals with another person. This is useful because it takes place in a sterile field. We may look at outside situations as well, but there we have to take into account that the person with whom he is dealing responds to him as his or her own object relations pattern dictates. The analyst does not respond according to her own needs, but in the service of the patient. This enables the patient to experience someone who does not play in with old patterns. It forces the patient to establish a new view—a new style of relating—because the analyst does not counterreact.

If So Much Is Determined So Early, Is All Lost?

No. Much depends on the child's endowment. A child possesses inborn capacity for adaptation, an activity that ensures survival. Therefore, even with poor maternal response, a child so endowed can find opportunities for development. Mr. Abel was not totally neglected by his mother, although he was not met with in an ideal way. This gave him a connection. Mr. Abel may be contrasted with a child who is so thoroughly neglected that he hardly has a sense that there are other persons—a narcissistic arrangement that constitutes a very severe and sometimes irreversible pathology.

Can Later Experiences Repair Earlier Damage?

Yes and no. Too much damage too early cannot be repaired. There are stages in development where more favorable experiences later make up for earlier unfavorable ones. One such situation is rapprochement. Mahler thought that a favorable rapprochement can make up for less than adequate earlier subphases of the separation-individuation process. I do not feel certain about this because experience is never erased. Perhaps one can say that the influence of negative experience in early life is diminished by favorable rapprochement.

Some mothers prefer some behaviors to others. For example, Mr. Abel's mother might have liked it when he began to verbalize. Again, this is only a working hypothesis based on his report that she was more responsive to verbalization than to activity. A child with a less responsive mother may have to work at eliciting a response. Sometimes that succeeds.

The Return to Home Base

Rapprochement is a return to home base. As a toddler explores his world sufficiently, he also becomes aware that he is really a very small person in a very large world. This brings about some anxiety. The natural response is to begin to cling more to mother, to be sure that she is still there after he has been more interested in exploration. If this need to return is met with a welcoming response, the child loses some of his fear and moves out once again into his circumscribed world. But if he is rebuffed, development is seriously retarded (Mahler et al. 1975; see Chapter 3).

It is not farfetched to speculate that Mr. Abel's mother did not welcome him back. We know that she was busy. Many such mothers are dismayed when their apparently independent toddler begins to "cling." I think that Mr. Abel had a less than satisfactory period of exploration followed by a rebuff when his mother was too busy to respond to his return to her.

What about Eliciting a Response?

The capacity to extract from the environment is inborn and exists in varying degrees in different individuals. A good extractor may be able to entice an indifferent mother to respond to his approaches. We can detect this in the treatment situation as the patient appears to seek out as much as he can get from the therapist or analyst. These are the kinds of cases that move along well because the patient knows from his early life that he is rewarded when he seeks developmental supplies.

Some patients who do possess the capacity to extract do not use it. Such patients can be educated in the therapeutic process. The ego is put to work when, in doing our part of the job, we refrain from doing too much for the patient.

How Much Is Too Much?

Doing too much for a patient is doing that which the person can do for himself. As the therapist allows space for the patient to fill, most patients will find the ability to fill it. The ego is strengthened by exercising.

Does Doing Too Much "Spoil" A Child?

We sometimes hear insensitive parents tell a child pejoratively that he is spoiled. Whose fault is that? A spoiled child is one who has been so overindulged that he develops a narcissistic view of himself in relation to the world. But that is not what the accusers mean. They usually mean that the child is not behaving as they would like. We do not spoil a baby by feeding him when he cries to announce that he is hungry, although it used to be thought so. Nor will he be spoiled if the mothering person responds to other cues. We may speculate that there was too little rather than too much response to Mr. Abel's cues when he was a baby.

Was Mr. Abel Spoiled?

No. He got too little of what laypersons call "attention" and we would call response to developmental need. He lived in a family that tolerated his presence and even liked him somewhat, but whose interest did not extend to responding flexibly to his changing developmental needs.

Can You Give an Example?

Although a baby cannot be spoiled, a toddler has to learn to live with others. He cannot outshout everyone else in the family. Imagine a family having dinner while the youngest of the children shouts, bangs his spoon, and in other ways makes things miserable for everyone else. He may not show the relief he feels at being stopped, but he will feel relieved nevertheless—relieved that an adult is in charge.

Was Mr. Abel's Mother Flexible Enough?

Probably not. A child has different needs at different stages of development. We have to think about whether this mother was able to alter her responses. I have already speculated that she was not flexible enough to respond to changing needs, to recognize the child's cues.

Can You Illustrate Cueing?

Cueing is reciprocal. Either partner in the mother–child dyad signals. If it is the child beginning to babble at the mother, for example, she babbles back. Then the child responds. The mother then might introduce a new sound and the child will pick that up. It becomes a mutually enjoyable game with important developmental implications for the child. He builds positive images of himself and of the other person as the enjoyment—the affective tone—registers the experience in his representational world.

Mr. Abel's mother, I believe, was too busy and too uninterested to spend time at that. Some mothers know it instinctively and enjoy it. We have to assume that Mr. Abel's experiences in this regard were on the meager side.

What about Changing Needs?

The obvious needs to be stated. We all know that a neonate changes physically from birth to 3 years of age and beyond. We have to consider that psychological needs differ with altering physique. When the child begins to crawl and then toddle, he has intense curiosity about everything, accompanied by a feel-ing of elation with the discoveries that become possible with attainment of the upright position. This is a time when the child needs freedom to roam, only to be restrained in situations of danger.

We assume that this patient's mother did not have time to follow him around and was not enchanted with his need to ex-plore. She had other things to do, and so she restrained him, I would suppose. The consequences are reflected in later life in his fear to venture.

The Role of the Father

In the second year of life, as the child's interests expand, the father is noticed more as a person different from the mother and more interesting in some ways. That tends to lure the child out of the tight relationship with mother that would retard develop-ment if it were to go on too long.

As gender differences are noted, the father is of major psy-chological importance to both a girl and a boy. For a girl he pro-vides an experience of how one relates to the opposite sex. For a boy he provides a model for identification.

We may be able to say that Mr. Abel's father, and to a lesser degree, his brothers, were there as objects for identification. They were not there actively enough. But Mr. Abel extracted whatever he could. Not having been met in this important developmental endeavor left him with a shaky gender identity because he had come to it almost by himself. One of the important diagnostic signs in this case is that gender identity, albeit shaky, was established.

Why Not a Role Model?

I used the term *identification* because it is more accurate. I have already said that I do not believe in the prevailing idea of a role model. That is good enough for the layperson. But as therapists and analysts we understand the importance of internalization and of the object world. This is more profound than role model because, with internalization, identification becomes part of the person's structure. That which once existed in the relational interchange is taken in to become part of the representational world. Therefore, a person does not model himself after another, but rather includes certain admired aspects of the other person in his self representation.

What Else Does the Father Do?

Long before he becomes an object for identification, he intrudes favorably in the young child's life. At first he is only vaguely distinguishable from the mother because, in infancy, need gratification dominates over object identification. Later, in the second year of life, the father plays with the child differently, roughhousing and tossing, providing an experience with someone different from the mother. The child becomes intensely interested in the father, and fantasizes about his life in the outside world. Thus the father lures the child out of the close relationship with the mother, thus expanding his experience of self in interaction with a wider world (Greenacre 1972, Mahler et al. 1975).

Mr. Abel's father was busy. He had a large family to support, worked hard and long, and was too tired to play with the child after work. He had already done that with the other boys and did not need more of it.

Sex Rears Its Head

Children are sexual beings. Humans are the only species that go through two phases of sexuality. Other mammals reach sexual maturity early and become able to mate. Humans, although they feel sexual, do not have the physical capability to engage in sexual intercourse until puberty. Even then, although early sexual behavior and parenthood abound, the cultural climate opposes it. And with good reason, for despite the physical capability, much more psychological development has to take place before a person is ready for mature sexual relationship and parenthood. We think of adolescence and young adulthood as developmental phases when the individual is preparing for love and work (Blanck and Blanck 1968).

That Mr. Abel could find a woman with whom to have a relationship was favorable, but there were many drawbacks. He was less interested in sex than in having someone. This connotes insufficient psychological separation from his mother, which impaired his ability to move on wholeheartedly in a new and nonfamilial relationship.

The Oedipus Complex

If the return to home base that I mentioned earlier is adequately met, the child moves on to form new and more sophisticated object relationships with the same objects. This seems strange. It can be explained by the fact that, although the objects in reality are the same, the psychological attitude toward them is different from before (see Chapter 14).

Was There Sexuality Before?

Yes. We are sexual beings from the start. But it takes different forms in infancy and young childhood. In infancy the child's interest is in his own body. He explores his body, finds that the genitalia give pleasure with touch, and begins to masturbate.

With the emergence into the world of sophisticated sexual interests that comes with psychological birth, the child shifts from narcissistic genital interest to interest in another person. Most children, in their approach to the oedipal level, turn their sexual interest to the parent of the opposite sex.

What Does Mr. Abel's Oedipal Arrangement Look Like?

The ideal developmental model would be a person who has had satisfactory experiences in every developmental phase leading up to the oedipal position and would negotiate that more complex matter with relative ease. There is no such person in reality. Therefore, we have to think about the degree of success or failure in the preceding developmental phases and how it facilitates or impairs the ability to negotiate the oedipal crisis.

Mr. Abel had developmental lacunae left over from inadequate preoedipal life. This increased the difficulty in dealing with oedipal demands and anxieties. He was not encouraged to venture, which I regard as a prime requisite for competent entry into the oedipal position. He was not well-enough separated from his preoedipal mother to be able to deal with her fully as an oedipal mother, that is, as an object of sexual desire. She remained too much an object with whom to merge.

His father did not lend himself to luring the boy out of his longing to be close to mother, a longing well-enough fulfilled by her at the phase-appropriate time. All in all, he approached the oedipal position on the "outskirts."

Where Should Treatment Be Addressed for Mr. Abel?

That depends on whether the treatment is to be psychoanalysis or psychotherapy. The ideal treatment for him would be psychoanalysis. It is beyond my scope here to describe how an analysis is carried out. There are many texts on the technique of psychoanalysis. One learns how to conduct an analysis not simply from texts but by full-fledged psychoanalytic training that includes personal analysis and supervised cases.

If it is to be psychoanalysis, we use free association, dreams, and the transference as the major tools that will reveal defenses, conflict, unconscious fantasies, and compromise formation. We would expect that Mr. Abel's characteristic pattern of object relations would determine the nature and quality of the transference. In the transference, the analyst will come to represent the preoedipal mother and the oedipal mother and father. The therapeutic objective would be resolution of the oedipal crisis.

In psychotherapy, the objectives would be similar for this case, but they would not all be reached. The transference would be used to reveal the self and object relations pattern. Perhaps by dwelling on that, more might emerge because of the nature of this case. For example, since we regard the oedipal position as an object relations factor, oedipal issues may arise and would be dealt with because Mr. Abel is essentially neurotic. That says that his ego can handle the conflict. In other psychotherapy cases the ego may not be capable of dealing with conflict. There one would focus on structure building (see Chapter 12).

I choose the object relations feature for psychotherapy with Mr. Abel as the one that holds the most promise for promotion of development and, perhaps, resolution of conflict.

11

Less Is More

Having described the second most desirable treatment for Mr. Abel, the present environment obliges me to discuss what can be done short of that. Lack of time cannot eliminate diagnosis, but with experience, a therapist becomes comfortable with a rough assessment to determine whether the patient is structured or understructured. That would, at least, keep the treatment from proceeding in the wrong direction. For emphasis, I repeat that we need to decide whether to build structure or to alter structure so that, however we proceed, we will not be stabbing in the dark.

Should We Begin with the Job Problem?

After all, that is the presenting problem. But, almost by definition, a patient can only present that which is conscious. The therapist listens beneath the manifest statement of the problem to try to grasp the latent content. Often, the presenting problem is a symptom. To deal with it at face value would deflect from the basic conflict.

The Several Ways of Skinning a Cat

A nonanalytic, logical person would take the presenting problem at face value and seize the obvious solution—advise the
patient to deal with the taunting by fighting back or advise him
not to mind it so much. I call these efforts "the good-neighbor
policy" because they are nothing more that what a friend or
good neighbor would suggest. A therapist is obliged to offer
more.

Why Not Treat the Symptom?

If symptom treatment could work, it would please the employer,
the insurance carrier, and perhaps even the patient himself.
It might make him happy in the short run. The behavioral approaches do treat the symptoms, reportedly successfully. But
the structure remains unaltered. Behavioral change can even be
harmful because it deflects from the real problem and discourages
the patient from seeking more profound treatment. "So what?" one
might ask, "It works." But the real problems—fear of aggression,
shaky gender identity, retreat from oedipal strivings—remain.

Why Worry about All That?

When a patient presents himself for treatment the therapist has
an obligation to be thorough. The patient who said that she only
wanted a little help is a case in point. A therapist is not a mer-
chant who sells what the customer asks for. We would not want
our doctors to declare that a tumor is benign because thorough
investigation is time-consuming and expensive. For Mr. Abel,
the therapist must see the underlying issues and treat as much of
it as time permits.

Symptom cure is harmful in another sense. Life is short. Mr. Abel is approaching middle age without a wife or children. He can live with his mother as long as she lives. When she dies, a therapist will have to treat depression in an elderly man.

What to Do When Time Is Limited?

Time limitation challenges the therapist's integrity. I have introduced the metaphor of psychoanalytic treatment as a full bucket. Limited sessions can only be drops in the bucket. But it is essential that they be the right drops. That leaves room for future treatment to continue adding more.

What Are the Right Drops in Six Sessions?

Regardless of the pressure of time, we need to know the structure. Treatment can begin immediately because some interventions can elicit information that both aids the diagnosis and performs some therapeutic work at the same time. The following condenses six sessions:

Therapist: Good morning. What brings you here?

Patient: They said you can help me with my problem. (Puts the initiative on someone else and does not reveal the problem.)

Therapist: Perhaps I can. (Does not promise.) What is the problem?

Patient: My coworkers won't leave me alone to do my work. (Externalizes the problem and also does not reveal very much.)

Therapist: Can you describe what happens? (Therapist has to prompt. I call this going uphill.)

Patient: Well, they call me names. I would like to know how to stop them. Can you tell me how?

Therapist: You would like me to tell you. (Refers to his passivity and puts the ball back in patient's court.)

Patient: Isn't that what you are supposed to do?

Therapist: I have to understand the problem better. Perhaps we can work out some ideas together. (Does not respond to the hostile tinge and offers a therapeutic alliance.)

Patient: One thing they pick on is that I still live at home. (The alliance takes hold. He offers a bit more information.)

Therapist: Does that make you angry? (Goes for the affect.)

Patient: I don't know. (Reveals unawareness of affect, a defense against his anger.)

Therapist: Perhaps it frightens you too much.

Patient: I did not think so, but now that you mention it, it is scary.

Therapist: Maybe it scares you to feel angry too.

Patient: I never thought of it that way. I always thought it was simply annoying.

Therapist: It would miserable to be frightened all the time. Are you more comfortable at home? (The therapist rewords the problem to highlight that home is a refuge from his anxiety and aggression. Also touched is his separation anxiety.)

Patient: Well, I do feel better when I am away from them.

(His ego does not allow him to acknowledge directly that home is a refuge. This is a good sign. He has masculine pride. Compare with the patient who said he is a baby and wants to sit on the therapist's lap.)

This illustrates how diagnosis and treatment can operate hand in hand. It opens the real issues, which are separation, blunted affect, and aggression. At the same time, it provides a glimpse of structuralization and ego competence.

What More Can Be Done in Six Sessions?

We can give him a taste of what it is like to work with a non-threatening person who does not judge him or insert her own ideas of how he should deal with his issues. Beyond that, we throw new light on the problem in the hope that that will intrigue him.

The Passive-Aggressive Ploy

I have heard many therapists refer to a patient as passive-aggressive. Never has this been without a pejorative connotation. Why do we dislike it so? It suggests that the patient is being sneaky, getting away with being hostile by taking refuge in passivity. I should like to suggest a different attitude. If we can train ourselves to listen to the affective tones, we might be able to view this behavior in a more sympathetic light. The patient who is so angry that it makes him anxious is not being sneaky. He is frightened and so does the best he can with it. He has to try to conceal his anger, even from himself. If he must do so in a passive mode for the time being, so be it.

About Passivity

This is something else that some therapists do not like. A senior analyst scornfully described an investment banker, who was known as a Wall Street killer. When he came for a consultation, he curled up in the chair in a fetal position. This reminds us once again of the patient who wanted to sit on the therapist's lap. One can become more neutral about it by taking the stance that passivity is the mode of the infant until he becomes a person in her own right. As Mahler has taught us, this takes three years. The toddler moves gradually from the passive to the active mode as he develops. Some observant mothers note the moment when the child grasps the feeding spoon and tries to feed himself. A major step into the active mode is identification with the aggressor when the child says *no* back to the person who has said it to him (Spitz 1972).

As a child becomes a person in the active mode, she enters the oedipal position. From wanting to be loved, he now offers active love to the parent of the other sex.

What If We Have Twelve Sessions?

Psychotherapy is not mathematical. We have no assurance that twelve sessions will do twice as much as six. In twelve sessions the therapist would be able to attain certainty about the diagnosis. Mr. Abel would be diagnosed as structured and the key problems—separation anxiety and fear of aggression—would be noted. One might be able to begin to help him become more alert to them. The value of more than six sessions is that he will acquire a greater appreciation for the nature of his problem. He will no longer seek symptom cure. He may find it worthwhile to think

of more prolonged therapy as an objective. The right drops will
have been added. More therapy will fill the bucket.

What If We Have Twenty Sessions?

Twenty sessions would give the therapy more quality time. By
quality I mean that the treatment would continue along the lines
dictated by the diagnosis rather than at random. More time, of
course, enables the therapy to place more drops in the bucket.
In twenty sessions Mr. Abel could realize that his anxiety keeps
him close to home and that he is at a loss at work because maternal protection is absent there.

Can Therapy Short of Analysis Go Further?

Yes. A very well endowed patient might be able to approach his
oedipal conflict in therapy short of analysis. The enormous anxiety that this would arouse can probably not be treated with infrequent contact. If the therapy is conducted at least three times
a week, one might think optimistically that the result would approach that of analysis proper. With a well-structured and well-
endowed patient, this is a theoretical possibility. But it is so rare
that I cannot recommend it for most patients. Note that I stress
the innate endowment, particularly the capacity to extract from
the environment.

What If Analysis Becomes Possible?

The diagnosis, separation anxiety as a regressive defense against
oedipal strivings in a well-structured patient, suggests a positive
prognosis. Another way of putting this will highlight the distinc-

tion between a neurotic and a borderline personality. Mr. Abel is neurotic and should be treated with the assumption that his structure can tolerate the anxiety that accompanies conflict. A borderline patient, less developed and less structured, would not present the same kind of conflict and would need to be treated in a way that would build structure. A middle-level borderline patient, and more certainly a high-level borderline might, with proper treatment, approach neurotic structure.

About Frequency

The therapist is faced with greater limitations than meet the eye when the number of sessions is limited. The tendency is to stretch them out over so many weeks. That is not likely to build as solid a transference as more frequent sessions. The therapist has to decide: Shall the patient be seen once a week for twelve weeks, or twice a week for six weeks?

There is no hard-and-fast rule. Such decisions have to be left to the therapist's "clinical feel." Then the decision will revolve around how best to maintain object connection and keep the threads of the treatment process alive. Freud deplored the "Sunday crust." He saw his patients six times per week and yet found that the one day without a session allowed time for repression to set in; the patient forgot on Monday what had been elicited on Saturday. How much more difficult is our task today.

12

The Borderline Conditions

The term *borderline* is a misnomer, yet it is so ingrained in the literature that we cannot change it; the best we can do is define it. Borderline does not refer to a single line, but rather resembles a geographic area with two borders—neurosis over the one border and psychosis over the other. The area in between these two pathologies is the borderline state.

Definition

I define the borderline state in developmental terms. According to Mahler, it represents failure to have completed the separation-individuation process and to have attained psychological birth. This contains within it the assumption that the object representations are experienced in some degree as part of the self representations. As I shall show, this is not easy to determine in the clinical situation, especially because we have no instruments for measuring the degree of separation. Nevertheless, the essence of treatment of the borderline, or understructured, personalities is to foster greater separation between the two sets of representations.

How Can We Tell?

We train ourselves to search it out. "Clinical feel" helps the therapist know whether the patient expects that the other person is to some degree part of the self. This is often detected more readily in a lower-level borderline patient who expects that the therapist will know what is on his mind. Such patients might experience some event in the time between sessions and expect that the therapist will know what has happened. Or the patient might be baffled within a session because he has not spoken and yet cannot understand why the therapist does not know what he wishes to convey. Or, "You're the doctor, you tell me the answer."

One patient often began a session with whatever took place as he was coming to the session. He continued in the same vein as though the therapist had been there. Often the content was about what happened at the office as he was leaving. Some patients notice what is happening on the subway or bus on the way to the session and begin with that.

With a higher-level borderline patient this matter is more difficult to detect because the patient's connection with reality is greater. Therefore, there might be wavering between expecting the therapist to know it all and the realization that the therapist has to be told. Here it is useful to refer to Spitz's third organizer of the psyche—semantic communication. The wavering patient has reached that organizer, but barely. He sometimes knows that he has to bridge the chasm between two persons, but sometimes wishes that it were not so.

The Contribution of Otto Kernberg

Kernberg divides borderline pathology into three levels—low, medium, and high. This division is extraordinarily useful in diagnosis as well as in determining the course of treatment. It addresses the fact that there is not a single condition that may be designated as borderline, but rather a range of conditions at varying levels within this broad area that we call borderline.

Kernberg does not speak of borderline *condition*, but rather *borderline personality organization*. The organization is analogous to neurosis in that there is a conflict and a distinct defense mechanism at play. That mechanism is *splitting;* the representations of the bad object are split off from the representations of the good object. The purpose of this defense is to keep the anger toward the bad object representations from damaging the good object representations. Later, I shall describe such a case, one in which the good and bad object representations are not fused.

I use the term *neurosis* as synonymous with *structured* and the term *borderline* as synonymous with *understructured*.

Diagnosis

Precise diagnosis of borderline conditions is more difficult than of neurosis because, in all neuroses regardless of individual variations, certain factors obtain. These are structuralization, internalization, conflict, defense, and compromise formation.

These factors vary more widely in the borderline states. Diagnosis must assess not only the degree of structuralization but also how much structure building is yet to be done, for building structure is the very task of the treatment. We are particularly concerned, in such cases, with level of object relations and with whether there is conflict and its nature—that is, whether the conflict is preoedipal, oedipal, or a mixture of both.

Oedipal Conflict

The oedipal conflict is the core conflict in neurosis. The core conflict in the borderline conditions is the failure to have negotiated the separation-individuation process successfully. To reiterate, such a person has not reached psychological birth, has not acquired a distinct identity, and has not reached a level of self and object relations that involves the very complex relationship toward both parents that the oedipal position demands. To put this another way, the individual is not psychologically free to enter into triadic object relations.

Nevertheless, oedipal issues are approached in some borderline cases. Then, the therapist is confronted with difficult diagnostic and treatment decisions. If possible, structure building should proceed, while oedipal matters should be postponed until the structure is more secure.

Are All Sexual Wishes Oedipal?

Infants and children have erotic feelings. Clinically, it is difficult to distinguish these from oedipal sexuality. One factor that may be helpful in making such distinction is that self relations are primarily narcissistic in young children. Exploration of the body and discovery of pleasurable genital sensations are not to be construed as object related.

Preoedipal Conflict

Preoedipal conflict prevails in the understructured patient. Conflict is between the self representations and the object representations, between wish to unite and wish to separate, between love and hate.

In smooth development, where self and object representations are relatively clearly delineated, the individual can enter the heart of the oedipal conflict. It is hardly possible for such ideal arrangement to obtain. But the structured patient, as compared with the understructured, has more or less resolved preoedipal conflict between the self and object representations in the dyad and is better able, then, to cope with triadic conflict.

Defense

It is useful to review the distinction between defense and defense mechanism as it pertains to the borderline conditions. A defense mechanism is employed by a competent (structured) ego as response to a signal of anxiety. That means that anxiety, the result of conflict, is experienced not in toto but as a signal to employ defense. The usual defense mechanisms in neurosis were enumerated by Anna Freud (1936). The list is not exhaustive. It includes repression, regression, reversal, isolation, reaction-formation, turning against the self, and perhaps sublimation. We are uncertain about whether sublimation is a mechanism of defense or a normal deployment of drive.

Defense, as contrasted with defense mechanism, is used by the less structured patient who does not have those discrete mechanisms available. Such patients will use whatever comes handy. Many borderline patients are fearful of wished-for merger and therefore defend against closeness by distancing and by use of anger as a defense.

In neurosis, defense mechanisms are readily available. This may be compared with a well-equipped army that has the most efficient weapons. The understructured personality must resort to less competent defense such as sticks and stones rather than modern firearms.

What Do Borderline Defenses Look Like?

Distancing keeps the therapist at arm's length. This is to prevent wished-for merger. One low-level borderline patient, close to psychosis, moved the chair close to the door of the consultation room, as far away from the therapist as possible. Most low-level and middle-range borderline patients are not so literal about distancing. They do it by appearing remote, far away. They fear that the therapist will become so close that merger involving loss of identity will be the outcome. Sometimes they verbalize this. "You will envelop me, swallow me up." Such patients require a long time with the therapist before they come to the realization that it is not the therapist's need to envelop them, but that they are defending against their own wish.

Anger is another common form of defense in understructured patients. This is complex because such patients are angry for many reasons, some justifiable. Here I am discussing anger as a defense, as a means of keeping the therapist at bay.

Those low-level borderlines who do not defend even in these primitive ways are more disturbed and need special help in keeping them from decompensating altogether. The man who wanted to sit in the therapist's lap might have been told that the therapist is not his mother. That would be another way of holding him to reality.

Psychoanalysis or Psychotherapy?

Most ambulatory borderline patients who come to our consultation rooms tend to cluster in the middle range and need psychotherapy rather then psychoanalysis. In long-term treatment it is possible that such patients will become analyzable. Low-level borderline patients need much help in structure building to develop a competent ego with functions such as judgment and reality testing; they do not usually become analyzable.

Treatment Goals

Psychotherapy for the understructured personality is designed to build structure, to increase the degree of internalization, and to raise the level of object relations. These three features of development go hand in hand. The therapist deals with one or the other feature of this triad according to the material the patient provides in a given session. Focusing the treatment on one aspect of the triad inevitably affects the other two aspects, for they are not truly separable. This may be likened to weaving with three threads to form a pattern. In one session the separation feature is most prominent and is dealt with by using the material of the session to further separation. In another session structure building is the order of the day. In still another, the manner in which the patient deals with others as well as with the therapist is the prominent feature. The therapist picks up each thread as it presents itself and bears in mind that wherever this thread entwines it will inevitably affect the nature of the others.

Prognosis

Some middle-range and high-level borderline patients can be helped to become analyzable after preliminary psychotherapy that promotes development. Since they possess a greater degree of structuralization than lower-level borderlines, they have less developmental distance to travel.

The low-level borderline patient may be helped considerably, especially if treatment is long term. High-level borderline patients are, by definition, close to neurosis and may demonstrate some neurotic conflict. A skillful analyst who attends to structuralization may analyze such a patient with some alteration in technique when regression dictates departure from strict analytic procedure.

Clinical Illustrations

A patient in analysis for almost a year regressed too far. The analyst was alerted to this by a dream. The patient dreamed that some people sunning on a beach changed into seagulls and flew away.

The analyst became concerned about the change in species. This does not happen in more competent structures. The patient described having seen people and seagulls at the beach. In her dream, she confused the two species. Reparative work had to done to stem the regression. In earlier times, when analysts knew less about the borderline conditions, they resorted to the rather desperate device of having the patient sit up to try to stem the regression. This is no longer necessary. We need only bring the patient back to reality. We don't analyze the dream; instead, asking "Do you really think people can become birds?" would begin the repair by stressing the reality. Later, one might look for where in her history the object representations were so hazy that she thought they could fly away.

Another patient was diagnosed as a medium- to high-level borderline, with inability to retain the representation of the object in his or her absence. That diagnosis was based on assessment of the patient's relationships outside as well as within the therapy. He was in his second marriage and looking around for a third wife if the present one were to displease him. This alerted the therapist to two interrelated matters: (1) objects are interchangeable—if one displeases, there can be another; and (2) the good and bad objects are not fused into representations of a whole person. That makes it easy for him to discard the bad object and seek another good object.

This dictates that part of the treatment is to help him realize that both good and bad experiences emanate from a single person and that, where good experiences predominate, one accepts the imperfections for the greater good of becoming able to love.

We do this by shaping the material that comes to hand. This man presented daily complaints about his wife. One time she was too slow getting ready to go out. Another time she forgot that he likes cream in his coffee. His anger was out of proportion to her shortcomings. As he talked about having an affair with another woman who presumably would please him more, the therapist used the material to help him begin to think about his search for the perfect woman. This tapped his latent reality testing. He was able to go along with the question about whether such perfection really exists and, beyond that, would he be happy with it. "No," he responded, "She would suck me in." Here we see in action the wish for perfect understanding and fear of wished-for merger were there to be such a perfect partner. By the response, we see that he is able to choose the more progressive direction. Then he is ready for the next step without much intervention by the therapist. Realizing that the perfect, good object would make him anxious, he began to consider taking the bad with the good. In normal development the two sets of object representations are fused as the developing child realizes that good and bad experiences emanate from the same person.

With this adult patient, the objective is to help him become able to love another person despite her human flaws. We are reminded here that Freud said in 1914 that we must love in order not to fall ill.

Another patient began treatment by defending against closeness with hostile remarks designed to keep the therapist at bay. "You look lousy today," "I don't like what you are wearing," and "You look tired" were some of the ways he began sessions. After this went on for a while, the therapist invited him to look at it and try to describe it. He said, "I am taking a shot at you." This is a way to get the observing ego to work in the treatment.

Note that the negative tinge came at the beginning of a session, as though to warn the therapist, "Keep your distance." As the therapist gently urged him to look at these "shots" each time, he began to realize that he needs them to maintain distance from an otherwise positive transference. That is a favorable sign; there is defense. The patient is capable of loving feelings, but fears them. Love threatens to lead to merger, and so whatever developmental gain has been reached must be maintained.

How Do You Interpret Such a Defense?

Interpretation is not appropriate in the borderline conditions. In the better-structured patient there is sufficient distance between self and object representations for the therapist to be able to make an interpretation across the chasm of separateness. The understructured patient cannot receive such communication from

another person because the therapist is not experienced as a separate, whole, other person. I have described this in Chapter 6.

> A patient has a long-term mistress and moves readily
> from wife to mistress as his feelings dictate. When one dis-
> pleases him, he goes to the other. He has not fused the good
> and bad objects into representations of a whole, separate,
> other person. That, then, will have to take place in the trans-
> ference. The technical difficulty is to prevent the patient
> from fleeing treatment when he feels displeasure with the
> therapist. It is contraindicated to elicit negative feelings too
> soon. One does not overlook them, but postpones by keep-
> ing them in a holding pattern. At the beginning of treatment,
> the patient's need for the therapist solidifies to form the
> positive side of the transference.

None of this is interpreted. In Chapter 6 I explained why
the transference of the understructured patient is uninterpretable.
Here I wish to convey that one focuses on allowing positive
cathexis of primary objects to repeat in the transference before
eliciting the negative affect. The patient fears that negative affect will destroy the object, and needs the solid base of a positive transference within which negative feelings may be risked.
    Negative feeling will surely come, but the positive becomes
"money in the bank." It prevents the patient from becoming
overwhelmingly anxious about destroying the therapist. Ultimately, he will come to realize that he has both kinds of affect
toward the same person.
    This is the process of fusion of the good and bad object
representations that takes place, normally, in childhood. It is a
developmental milestone when the child realizes that both good
and bad affective experiences emanate from the same person. If

the positive predominates, smooth development proceeds, now in the continuing relationship with the fused object representations. In the history of most, or all, borderline patients, negative experience predominates, rendering fusion impossible because, in the interest of adaptation, the child has to cling to the representation of a good object.

How Can You Deal with It, Then?

As already illustrated, it is best to take one's time, to tolerate it, to look for ways to ask the patient about it. Especially important is to appreciate it. Be glad that the patient is defending himself. Without defenses the person would be unable to function.

As the boundary between self and object representations becomes more distinct, one might strive for self interpretation. One leads the patient to it gently. "Why do you say that?" will not usually bring an immediate answer. We have to be careful not to seek rewards. This patient took his time, justifying what he said with reference to reality. "You really do look lousy today." With time and patience he became able to look beyond the reality toward why he needed to begin each session with a negative tinge. Ultimately he understood that he needed to create emotional distance.

Treatment Plan

The therapist determined that less than three times per week would retard work on this patient's level of object relations. Simply put, he would forget the therapist as a potential transference object because of his inability to retain a constant representation of the object. Failure of object retention was caused in large measure by a developmental deficit plus intense anger that tended to erase object images. In this case as in many, the mother of his early childhood did impair the normal progress of the separation-individuation process by maintaining too much closeness as the child's developmental thrusts threatened to take him away from her.

How Do You Know That?

Two ways of knowing that are available to the therapist. One is the patient's behavior with the therapist and with outside persons. The other is the life history. As the patient told about his childhood, it became clear that his mother could not tolerate his separating thrusts. He gave examples. His mother did not allow him to go to school without her when he was old enough to go with the group of children who lived on the block. For a long time in treatment he feared that the therapist would need him too much.

In many cases that fear is a deterrent to the patient's willingness to accept frequent contact. A patient may defend in other ways—time, money, distance from the therapist's office, and the like. These are not easy to overcome. This is another place where we have to be patient and cautious—cautious to avoid giving the patient reason to fear we need him too much.

Therapeutic Decision

Psychotherapy was directed at raising the level of object relations, with knowledge that structuralization and development as a whole were part of this goal. Although anger served as a defense against too much closeness, it did not serve him well. It impaired retention of the representations of the object; he erased the object images and then suffered object loss. The beginning of treatment, therefore, was directed toward helping him acquire a more stable internalized self and object relationship. Only when it became stable and durable was it safe to deal with the anger as reality as well as defense.

What to Do about the Anger?

Much of this patient's anger stems from his mother's psychological restraint. The developing child uses the aggressive drive in the service of separation. When this is thwarted, that benign use of the aggressive drive turns to anger. This would have to be dealt with some later time. The first order of business was attention to the use of anger as a defense against closeness.

Frequency

While the desirable frequency of attendance is four or five times per week for the psychoanalysis of neurosis, the understructured patient may be seen less frequently. This is because the neurotic patient can recover from the inevitable regression in the treatment session, while recoverability is less reliable in the borderline patient. It is not desirable to allow the borderline patient to regress to the point where she loses sight of reality. Three times per week seems to be a good rhythm for many borderline patients. I have said that I do not favor once-a-week treatment because the very important factor of maintaining object connection is lost with infrequent sessions.

What about Reality?

This question asks about external matters. The patient lives too far away to attend frequently; her job requires out-of-town trips;

the person cannot afford frequent sessions. We need to examine the reality that the patient presents. How real is it? Is it being used in the service of defense because fear of closeness dominates in so many of these cases? If this fear could be diminished, would the patient then be able to overcome the reality as an obstacle to treatment?

What about the Financial Reality?

I have trouble with that. In a favorable economy, there are choices. A patient who has a second home, a car, and a boat, who goes on trips for vacation, can pay if she forfeits one of those luxuries. The person who cannot pay because income is too low is in a different category. Often it is a matter of motivation. There is nothing like good experience in treatment to boost motivation. Also, more often than not, job promotion comes with therapeutic gain.

13

Primary Prevention

A number of scattered programs are in effect for the treatment—not prevention, but treatment after the fact—of neurologically and physically handicapped children. Here I am proposing that we attend to normal children to anticipate developmental problems before they occur. I base my position on·the theme I have propounded throughout—that inadequacy in one phase of development impairs adequate attainment of the next phase.

The discoveries of the child observationalists are useful not only in treatment of children and adults, but in prevention of potentially pathological situations in the course of development. Because the first three years of life are crucial to building structure, including self and object relations, and because those developmental years, if adequate, lead to psychological birth, we may now use the observational studies and their theoretical conclusions to help parents, teachers, and other caregivers to provide a head start for the child from birth on.

I use the term *head start* advisedly. Spitz (personal communication) believed that the Head Start program for prekindergarten children is too late. The child, literally, has to be started up at birth. Although I have made much of the capacity to extract from the

environment, even the best-endowed child cannot extract emotionally nurturing supplies if they are not there. One patient who
was born to a depressed mother extracted her affective state and
suffered a lifelong depression.

I shall follow this developmental process in a hypothetical
child from birth on. I begin by recapitulating Hartmann's concept of adaptation, which is the reciprocal relationship between
the organism and its environment—the encounter of the neonate
with the mothering person. Input comes from both sides. The
mothering person brings her nurturance and loving response
tailored to what she learns about this particular child as she tends
to him. The child brings his innate endowment, including capacity to extract from the environment. The first task of this mother–
child pair is to begin to know each other—to find a way of fitting together. Hartmann regarded fitting together as even more
important than adaptation. It appears to me that he made an il-
logical distinction. It is more appropriate, I believe, to regard
fitting together as the first adaptive step. The head start, then, is
to establish a good fit from the start and to pursue the interaction in an action–reaction–action cycle.

What Is This Good Fit Like?

It is wordless. The fit is established as both partners in the dyad
reach out to each other affectively. On the mother's side, she is
enraptured with the child and, while holding him, is oblivious
to all else. On the child's side, he is living in the primary process and in his experience the mother is part of him. This is depicted in dozens of paintings and statuary because artists can
express the rapture displayed on the mother's face as she holds
the contented child.

How Does a Mother Learn about Her Child?

Mutual cuing is the critical activity that accompanies physical care. As the mothering person feeds, bathes, diapers, plays with, and soothes the child, each partner cues the other. The holding and looking contain affective communications that both partners decipher as they get to know each other. Shortly, an object relations sequence begins to develop; the child becomes the particular child of this mother. The same mother with another child will be different because the other child will bring his own unique input, causing both mother and child to interact in a new way.

The Role of Affect

As we learn more about the affective climate within which the child flourishes, both physically and psychologically, we appreciate Emde's (1999) finding that affect is the warp that holds together the otherwise disparate aspects of development. Affect prevents development from becoming chaotic. It is conveyed back and forth between mother and child in their everyday encounters.

The Early Hazards

I have described the ideal climate within which the normal child will flourish. What if the climate is less than ideal? The harried, indifferent, depressed, or psychotic mother who does not respond to the child's cues is depriving the child of developmental opportunity, particularly in the area of building self and object relations.

For contrast with the ideal, let us visualize an indifferent mother who cuts corners. She gives the infant a propped bottle,

depriving the child of physical and affective contact. She regards him as a "good baby" if he sleeps much of the time and
does not complain. Perhaps this was so with Mr. Abel, whose
mother was not totally indifferent but preoccupied with other
matters. Does this kind of start diminish expectation? Would
Mr. Abel have been more ambitious if he had been started up
more enthusiastically?

Are You Talking about Bonding?

I have to say no. Bonding is a concept of British object relations
theory. It has entered the popular vocabulary where it means that
one person becomes affectively attached to another. That is so,
but developmental object relations theory goes further (see Chapter 5). The emphasis is not on attachment but on interlocking
of self and object images within the evolving representational
world.

I want to stress the importance of the interlocking or intertwining of the self and object images because the mutual cuing
and responding in action–reaction–action cycles is so much more
than mere attachment. It involves the developing child's taking
part of the mothering person into his mental representations and
making them his own as he goes on to establish his own identity.

Let us think about the infant who summons the mother by
crying upon awakening. The mother's footsteps are heard even
before she arrives. The infant, having experienced being attended
repeatedly, begins to organize the pattern: cry, footsteps, being
lifted out of the crib and seizing the breast as it is offered, looking at the mother's face while nursing. Being held snugly and
being gratified also become part of the gestalt as does the affect
that joins mother and infant at this interval that is so happy for

both of them. Satisfied, the infant is held, bubbled, diapered, all the while interacting with the mother as they cue each other. The infant is returned to the crib to sleep contentedly.

What Has Happened?

The experience of self and object in affective harmony and responding one to the other builds images of self and other that, at first, are experienced as united. As these images gradually separate out with time and experience, they also become stable and thereby become representations that will last a lifetime.

This goes a bit beyond selective identification, although it includes it. As the separation-individuation process proceeds, functions as well as representations of the object become transferred to the self representations. (Transfer of function is described in Chapter 4.)

What Do You Mean by Primary Prevention?

To illustrate this, we may follow a child though all of the developmental phases described in Chapter 4. Combining the conclusions of Spitz and Mahler, whose work is complementary, we are able to examine the mother–child interaction at any phase of development. A keen and educated observer of mother–child interaction can detect disequilibrium in the relationship before it impairs the child's development.

Example 1

In extraordinarily pathogenic situations, the child fails to reach the smiling response. It can be remedied if there is intervention before distorted development goes too far. Here once again I am using Spitz's finding that distortion in one phase also distorts the manner in which the next phase will be reached.

The mother may be taught to hold the child more if she is physically and psychologically able. If the mother is incompetent—ill, depressed, psychotic, alcoholic, on drugs, or absent— another caregiver must take over quickly. Babies hospitalized for failure to flourish respond remarkably to nurses who hold them. That can only be temporary, however. Hospitalization is an emergency measure and has the disadvantage of loss of continuity of connection with the same object. Changes in caregivers impair smooth progress through the three organizers (see Spitz, Chapter 3) and the separation-individuation process (see Mahler, Chapter 3). This is because mental representations of a consistent object cannot build where the objects change. I am beginning to suggest outside intervention and I shall elaborate on that.

Example 2

A child reaches the second organizer in Spitz's series. He becomes wary of strangers. The mother wants him to be friendly and outgoing, to smile at everyone as he did a short while before. She feels that there is something wrong. Reassurance might reach some mothers who may be relieved to learn that the child's fear of strangers is a compliment to her. We have to take into account, however, that incompetent mothers may not care.

Example 3

As we have learned, Mr. Abel's parents planned a trip abroad when he was 9 months old, having already made reservations several months before. When the time came, they were a bit apprehensive, but decided to go nevertheless. They left the children with the aunt. Mr. Abel had just reached the level where the mother had become the "libidinal object proper" (Spitz). The parents were so intent on their trip that, despite apprehension, they found rationalizations: the child knows the aunt, he has no sense of time. They were almost "good enough" parents, but failed to listen to their apprehension.

This happens so frequently that it is worth examining in depth. Often the mother wants to leave the child because she senses that the child is developing and beginning to leave her. Such mothers experience this because the child has reached the subphase of differentiation in Mahler's scheme. If the mother has enjoyed a cuddly baby who is close to her, physical as well as psychological changes render the child no longer the baby who molded to the mother's body. Now the musculature and burgeoning interest in a wider range of the object world make the child more separated. The mother feels rejected and rejects the child in turn.

How Can This Be Prevented?

If there had been a regular consultation for the course of the child's development, the parents could have been encouraged to reconsider their decision to leave long before their trip. They would need to be told also that the child will have a severe reaction. In fact, this child refused to allow her mother to touch her for two days after the parents returned. The mother was stunned and, to her credit, said that she will never do that again. After that the child appeared to recover. Unfortunately, the break in the continuous building of object relations leaves a permanent scar. We cannot predict what will come of it because that will be different in different children. Lifelong separation anxiety? Distrust? Anger?

I believe that I am beginning to convey that primary prevention can consist of one small intervention that can have large consequences for a child's development.

Example 4

A mother and early practicing subphase toddler are at the beach. The child crawls away in a given direction. The mother turns him in another direction. He crawls that way. She turns him again. He crawls that way. She turns him again. At no time is the child in danger. He is beginning to have a severely impeded practicing subphase, likely to be subject to even more interference when he acquires upright locomotion. This is a problem in the mother. She needs to control the child's movements, perhaps especially as the child moves away from her independently. He will miss the elation of accomplishment, and the joy of discovery, and the healthy narcissistic pleasure that builds self-esteem, initiative, venturesomeness, and courage.

This mother's need to control is probably ego syntonic; she would not regard it as a problem for which to seek help. I shall go on to describe an ideal climate within which parents are accessible and find it socially and emotionally acceptable to be helped before the fact.

Example 5

A child has an adequate practicing subphase and enters the rapprochement subphase. He brings everything he can carry and places them in his mother's lap. Or he holds her leg while she is doing something else. The mother is dismayed because she enjoyed the practicing subphase when the child appeared to be independent. Now he is clinging. Feeling that this is not a favorable development, she rejects these advances as though to encourage independence, while the child needs this return to home base before venturing forth again.

It is difficult to explain rapprochement needs to a mother who does not understand it. As is true of stranger anxiety, the child appears to the mother to be behaving in a regressed way. She may even feel guilty that she has done something wrong to bring this about. A conscientious mother might respond to an explanation of the child's behavior and accept the child's need to cling to her for a short while.

The Affective Storms

This is commonly called the "terrible twos." It is difficult for parents to understand such tantrums. They might be able to tolerate it better if they could know what is going on in the child. The child is being torn by conflicting wishes. It can be described simply as wishing to come and go at the same time. It is more complex than that, but this oversimplified way of explaining it paints a picture of impossible ambivalence. With further development, more reality testing overcomes this ambivalence.

What about Day Care?

There are different kinds of day care. Children are left in private homes to be cared for, several at a time, or they attend day-care centers of varying quality. At its best, day care can be excellent for child and mother. Unfortunately, poor-quality day care is more prevalent. Quality is concerned with the ratio of caregivers to children, with the education and temperament of caregivers, and the equipment and setting of the facility. A good day-care center will have one caregiver with helper for not more than two babies under 1 year of age, a caregiver and helper for every four children in the second year, and for five or six children in the third year.

Babies and children under 3 years of age should not be in day care for more than four hours. This is not convenient for working mothers, but they are not to be encouraged to use day care as a substitute for home care. Children who are in day care for a seven-hour day or longer fall apart. They are overstimulated, overtired despite nap times, angry, and, especially, are strained to maintain mental representations of their objects. They fall apart when this retention fails. To the observer they are tired, cranky, and disoriented. Internally, they are experiencing object loss.

What Is a Working Mother to Do?

The best substitute is a grandmother. That is usually not possible these days when extended families do not live together. Next best is a caregiver who remains on the job, another requirement hard to fulfill. As a society we have not yet reached the point of accommodation for working mothers. Perhaps it will become something that is taken for granted in the future.

Take-the-baby-to-work arrangements are still not universal. The rare workplace that allows it is only adequate for young babies. Once they begin to crawl, the mother cannot do her work. On-site day care is a viable solution. There the mother can nurse the baby, or come to visit and play with an older child.

I am really discussing child care in the broadest sense—caring about the child. Do we care enough about our children to have better caregiving, better schools, better food for those who need it? Not yet.

When Should Primary Prevention Begin?

Ideally, it begins with the mother and father when they were infants. Good parenting begins with having been parented (Blanck 1987). Although that may not seem very practical because there is no going back, it is useful to think that having been parented provides the intuitive ingredient that makes it possible to become a competent parent. Good parenting can be taught to a willing parent. Developmental theory used for primary prevention can correct errors before impairment of development escalates.

How Should Parenting Be Taught?

It has already begun to be taught in the schools in a small way under the aegis of life skills. Sex education is combined with parenting education. Boys and girls are given hands-on instruction with dolls, may be taken to visit nurseries to handle real babies, or may be taught developmental theory in a simple way. Perhaps when they come to understand the profundity of child rearing there will less incentive to become teenage parents.

Wouldn't That Be Too Intellectual?

Yes. Boys and girls who have not been adequately parented may not catch on. Or, they may understand out of their own lingering needs. But I want to introduce an idea that we need to think about more. Since we are biologically equipped to become parents, is there not also some innate capacity to parent that accompanies the act of conception? This has not been researched, so I am proposing it without knowing the answer. It seems reasonable.

A New Profession

We have coaches and personal trainers for sports and body building. We have tutors for academic progress. But coaching for parenting is still a haphazard matter, sometimes done by nurses, nannies, grandmothers, pediatricians, and books aplenty. Yet there is not a profession with knowledge of developmental theory to guide a parent along. Yes, there are child therapists, usually consulted when something goes wrong. Often that is later than it needs to be, and it is not available to everyone.

If parent education for children in the schools is taken for granted as an essential part of education, coaching, too, at the time when these children become parents, will also seem to follow in the natural course of events.

Can a Person Be Made to Feel Maternal or Paternal?

Not everyone. I observed a group session for young men in prison for minor crimes, mostly petty theft and drug dealing. Those men had not had fathers and had no concept of fatherhood. Yet they all had children, some by several different women. When asked whether they would like to be with their children, they were baffled. They were unable to comprehend living with the mothers and children because they could not conceive of a place for them in a family. The group leader was hard pressed to explain why a child needs a father and what the father would gain from being with his child.

Would one teach them about the role of the father as I have described in discussion of the case of Mr. Abel? No. That would be akin to having an engineer explain the workings of a telephone when all one needs to know is how to dial. Perhaps these men are not teachable. Or, a few might be. It would be worth a try to have a coach be with them and help them interact in the way that would be age-appropriate for their child. Some of those men might be reachable if they could experience the pleasure of fatherhood.

How Would a Coach Intervene?

Too much has been said and written about how to do the right thing. That does not take into consideration that the right thing may not feel good to the parent. I have already illustrated one way to coach by showing the parent that it can be pleasurable.

It is believed that infants cannot be rewarding—that they require much and give little. The smiling response may not excite a mother who is in a depression. There the coach can intervene actively with the baby. That would not cure the mother's depression. But it would avert the irreparable consequence to the child of trying to extract and being able only to extract the mother's depressed affect.

A patient was born after his father's death. Clearly, the mother was in mourning. In the course of his therapy as an adult, it was found that his mother never stopped mourning and that it turned into lifelong depression. He was able to function moderately well in his profession, but he was totally unable to have a love relationship with a woman. His overall affective state was a moderate depression. He wanted the therapist to join him. It was distressing to him to realize that the therapist was not depressed. The question arises: Would the therapist be able to lure him into experiencing her normal affect? As it turned out, this was effective to a limited degree only, for it entailed separating from his maternal representations with whom he did have an affective tie, albeit a pathological one. To lure him away completely would have entailed object loss. A compromise was reached whereby he was sometimes able to identify with the therapist's affect and sometimes not.

What Could Primary Prevention Have Done?

Indication for intervention was clear during the mother's pregnancy because of her husband's death. A coach could have prepared the mother for the arrival of the baby and could have determined the extent to which the mother would need help for her depression and for getting the child "started up."

How Can a Depressed Mother Be Helped?

A disturbed or depressed mother needs help for her illness, and that should be provided. Meanwhile, we do not want the child to suffer irreparable damage. This is a place where a coach may have to take over a bit more than simply teaching or demonstrating. Although I have shown that it would be good to teach through showing how pleasurable parenting can be, a depressed mother, by definition, cannot experience pleasure. Early quality day care might offer the child an opportunity to experience objects with normal affect while the mother is being treated for her depression.

Isn't That Psychotherapy?

That depends on the definition. There can be no doubt that the two professions would overlap. I am not suggesting that a psychotherapist be a coach, or that a couch learn psychotherapy. I am advocating two different skills.

What Is the Difference?

A psychotherapist needs to be trained in psychoanalytic developmental theory, to understand unconscious fantasy, to be analyzed himself, and to have carried cases under supervision. The psychotherapist's job is to repair pathology.

A coach needs to know the findings of the child observationalists and to be able to intervene actively in anticipation of pathological consequences before they occur. The coach's job is to prevent pathology.

What Would a Coach Need to Know?

Hands-on child development. This would be different from training in child therapy. Therapy is corrective; coaching is preventive. A coach would go into the home before critical stages in development and steer the parents in the right course. This, of course, would be difficult to sell because we would have to be very convincing about avoiding problems before they become evident. Like vaccines that prevent illness before it occurs, we cannot prove that the illness would come about without it. Yet, vaccines are generally accepted. If the infant and mother are not interacting favorably in the early weeks, the child will not organize to the point of the smiling response. Can we explain that the smile may not come about before that serious developmental failure occurs?

What about Other Theories?

Different and sometimes competing theories exist now and will continue to be elaborated in the future. Some are fads that will

pass; others are to be taken seriously. I have presented the theory
of psychoanalytic developmental psychology. A training program for coaches will probably have to be eclectic. The coach
will choose the theory that appears most compelling.

Isn't Your Idea Utopian?

Of course it is. It is as utopian as good health care for all, good
food and housing, and good schools.

14

Is There Life after Age Three?

To do justice to the developmental phases following the separation-individuation process would require an entire volume on each phase. Some of this work has been done—by Blos (1962) on adolescence; by Blanck and Blanck (1968) on marriage as a developmental phase, and by Benedek (1959) on parenthood as a developmental phase. However, these contributions deal with the particular developmental phases favored by the authors and therefore are not part of a sequential presentation of all of the developmental phases from birth to old age. Erikson (1959) has described a life cycle that is similar to but not precisely the same as the theory I am following here.

Each phase is worthy of in-depth consideration. I shall outline each one here in sequence to show how one is dependent on the success of the phase that precedes it if it is to fulfill its developmental purpose. I shall also touch on the particular developmental tasks of each phase, some in review. By so doing, those areas of developmental theory that call for further investigation will be highlighted.

The Oedipus Complex

Between the ages of 3 and 6, if structure is relatively complete, the child enters the oedipal position. Freud discovered the Oedipus complex in his self-analysis. He designated it as the core conflict of neurosis. The source of the conflict is that sexual desire usually focuses on the parent of the opposite gender while the same-gender parent is regarded as a rival. This is the central feature in neurosis, and attains special importance in psychoanalysis proper.

The myth upon which Freud based his discoverey has it that the son, Oedipus, unknowingly (unconsciously) killed his father and married his mother. A myth represents universal truth. Thus, Sophocles has dramatized everyone's unconscious fantasy. The Greeks who watched Sophocles's drama enacted on the stage could connect with it because it represented their own unconscious fantasies, as it does ours. The aftermath is that Oedipus, upon discovery that he has had sex with his mother, destroys his eyes, a symbolic castration.

How Does It Look?

Freud depicted the Oedipus complex as triangular. I have wondered about his geometry (Blanck 1984). If the triangle is equilateral, it is a poor depiction of the position of the child, for it places her as equal with the parents. If it is an isosceles triangle, it places the child too far away from the parents. I have suggested that we diagram this complex relationship as a straight line, with one parent at either pole. The child moves along the line as the feelings about each parent fluctuate, at one moment close to mother, at another moment closer to father, sometimes in the middle.

With this diagram, we can depict the wavering loyalties of the child as he approaches the oedipal position, moving in his object relations interests from one parent to the other. In most circumstances, the child alights on sexual interest in the parent of the opposite gender.

In his description of the complete Oedipus complex, Freud included a negative oedipal position. He regarded that as developmental; he thought that it precedes the positive position. There the child prefers the same gender parent.

The negative oedipal position can also be defensive. Freud (1911) illustrated the defensive feature in his discussion of paranoia. The defensive formula is "I do not hate you and want to be rid of you; I really love you."

How Does It Come About?

The oedipal position is arrived at, ideally, by a child who has attained psychological birth and has acquired identity. We now think that there are several rounds of the oedipal crisis—in early childhood, in adolescence, in young adulthood, in marriage, in parenthood. In good development, the oedipal conflict wanes at each round.

Whether a child arrives fully at the oedipal position in the first round depends upon how much that child is free of or burdened by preoedipal, separation-individuation issues. This conflict, involving as it does complex attitudes toward both parents and one's own sexuality, is difficult at best. It is endured most competently if not contaminated by issues that should have been resolved earlier; it is rendered more difficult if preceding issues intrude upon and deflect from the child's developmental competence.

How Is It the Core Conflict in Neurosis?

If preoedipal life has gone relatively well, structure is formed. Although we now consider also that there can be preoedipal conflict, that is of a different nature. It consists of conflict between self and object representations as the separation-individuation process proceeds. With structuralization, conflict exists within the structure. The id wishes, the superego forbids. This conflict is mediated, not resolved, by the ego as it defends against the anxiety that the conflict creates. In so defending, the ego negotiates a compromise between id and superego, forming an uneasy peace that we call neurosis.

Perhaps all persons, even the less structured, approach the oedipal position in some way. This is controversial. Can a psychotic structure entertain oedipal strivings? I think we have to distinguish between primitive, physical erotic interest, on the one hand, and object-related interest at the oedipal level.

The Object Relations Factor

The oedipal position, after all, is an object relations position. It has been described classically in drive theory terms: libido alights upon the parent of opposite gender. As part of the psychosexual progression from oral to anal to phallic, it is designated as the precursor of genitality. Genitality, Freud thought, is attained only after puberty when sexual intercourse becomes possible.

Drive theory alone, however, provides only partial descriptions that do not do justice to the totality of the oedipal position. They have especially come into question because it is doubted whether there is a phallic phase in girls (Edgcombe and Burgner 1975).

To regard the oedipal position in object relations terms broadens our view of it, for it truly represents the feelings and attitudes toward each parent. In ordinary circumstances, these feelings are loving, negative, erotic, and fearful.

What Do You Mean by Approach?

Not everyone arrives at the oedipal position in the same way, at the same time, or in the same place. When burdened by inadequate preoedipal experience, some persons "limp" into the oedipal position. The complete Oedipus complex may be visualized as a target with outer circles. Some persons reach the outer circles, but not the bull's eye. This attempts to describe how they approach the oedipal position but may not enter it fully. That has important implications, especially for psychoanalytic treatment where the Oedipus complex is so central in neurotic structure.

How Does It End?

I have noted that mental representations are never lost, but remain fixed for life. Therefore, we may speak of residual oedipal desire permeating all subsequent developmental phases. This implies that the developmental task of each phase is to carry the individual ever closer to a resolution that, in the final analysis, is only relative. In that sense, it might be more accurate to speak of attenuation rather than resolution.

Whenever we have several terms that attempt to define the same matter, we are entitled to think that there is uncertainty. The solution, or resolution, of the Oedipus complex is written about in terms such as repression, waning, and dissolution. This reflects uneasiness about whether it is ever completely laid to rest (Blanck 1984, Loewald 1980). The classical position that the oedipal conflict involves murder and incest leaves too little room for resolution, or as Loewald has said so felicitously, for waning.

In the usual family, the child comes to love both parents long before the oedipal period. Sexual desire for the parent of the opposite gender may overshadow, but does not obliterate, love for the same-gender parent. Jacobson provides a more loving solution. The child substitutes identification for rivalry. Love for the same-gender parent wins out over rivalrous feelings. By means of identification with the beloved same-gender parent, the child abandons rivalrous wishes in favor of becoming like that parent.

Is It Real?

The question arises, when a 3-year-old wishes to kill her rival, does she know the meaning of death? Do boys and girls really believe that the wish to kill the parent of the same sex disposes of her or him forever, or is it the whim of the moment? Will the child want the parent back at another moment? Adults have problems accepting death even though they know that it is irreversible. Does a 3-year-old know that death is forever? Or, rather, in the heat of her desire, does she want her mother out of the way for the moment, only to want her to return when there is need for her? Who will lull the child to sleep if her mother is gone forever? I am suggesting that the wish of the moment is one thing—that at another time of the same day regression to need for maternal comfort can take over.

The boy's regression is similar, but is often mistaken as oedipal because, in his case, the need is for the parent of the opposite gender. In that regressed state, however, it represents need for the preoedipal mother. We normally long for the comfort of the preoedipal mother in times of distress. Mahler said we long for the mother of symbiosis from the cradle to the grave.

Latency

Latency is thought to offer a respite from conflict so that the child's energy may be devoted to learning. The elementary school years are believed to be free of sexual and aggressive wishes for the time being. That, it appears, is an ideal. Returning to the supposition that inadequate development in one phase burdens development in the next phase, we are permitted to wonder whether there can be so perfect a separation-individuation phase, and so perfect an oedipal resolution, that the child can truly enter latency in its literal meaning—that sexual and aggressive wishes are latent.

Much depends on balance. An inadequate completion of the separation-individuation process suggests failure to acquire identity, failure to attain object constancy, and incapacity to deal with oedipal issues even if they arise. These intrusions prevent the so-called latency child from the temporary peace that latency implies. If latency is adequate, there is a respite from conflict until emergence of puberty.

Puberty

Gender identity is established in four stages. First there is an inborn primary masculinity or femininity. Second, the parents assign gender to the infant, usually in conformity with the physical attributes of the child. Third, the child in the second year of life himself identifies with the parent of the same sex. Fourth, puberty renders gender identity decisive.

It is beyond my scope to enter the debate about whether homosexuality is a normal alternative. I must also omit discussion of the many pathologies that derive from uncertain gender identity and uncertain body image, such as fetishism and the eating disorders. I do wish to note, however, that the dramatic bodily changes at puberty make it difficult for the developing child to deny his or her gender without grave distortion of the reality. If doubt existed as the result of failure to have attained solid gender identity in the preceding stages of gender identity acquisition, puberty brings with it confusion, conflict, and opportunity for pathological fantasy. Such intrusions impair the use of puberty as yet another developmental phase—one in which gender identity and further identification with the parent of the same sex are solidified.

If puberty is attained in orderly sequence, relatively unburdened by incompletion of the phases that precede it, it may be used to prepare the individual for his or her future as an adult.

Usually girls attain puberty earlier than boys. As their bodies round out, as they grow breasts, as they reach menarche, opportunity for fantasy abounds. Fantasy can be used normally to project oneself into the future as a woman in preparation for adulthood. It can be used pathologically to deny bodily changes, to reject them, to be at odds with the reality—at odds because bodily changes cannot be halted or reversed. Girls also have to deal with blood. Here is an opportunity to fantasy about damage, injury, castration, pain, and, normally, eventual motherhood. The girl who is satisfied with herself—that is, possessed of healthy narcissism—welcomes puberty as the arrival of womanhood.

Boys generally mature later than girls and more secretly at first. The first signs of puberty—growth of pubic hair and the drama of the emission—is not apparent to the outside observer as are the first signs in the girl, such as breast growth. So a boy experiences his manhood in a way that is not noticed by others. Only with the external changes that are so slow in coming must he face the world as a man. Again, as with the girl, denial of the reality incurs grave psychological consequences.

For both sexes, puberty brings sexual wishes to the fore once again. If there has been true latency, this represents an awakening. I have already expressed doubt about whether latency can be so complete. But with puberty, sexual interest, including oedipal wishes, become powerful because consummation has become possible and must be delayed. It must be delayed because physical maturation and psychological development do not proceed in parallel. The body may be ready for sexual intercourse and parenthood, but the psyche is not. Premature sexual relations, even though the body is ready, may also impair phase-appropriate development. It curtails the use of puberty and even adolescence for education and development toward adult responsibilities.

Adolescence

Each phase of life has its phase-specific developmental tasks. These are best performed when relatively unencumbered by incompletion of the tasks of the preceding phase. Adolescence involves oedipal, separation-individuation, and identity tasks. Oedipal issues reach another step in the waning process, aided by the physical capacity to seek relationships outside the family. Separation-individuation, which is never complete, goes through another round in adolescence when the person experiences conflict about self-realization versus parental ties (Blos). Identity includes final acceptance of one's gender, the role that it is to play in the person's life, and how it relates to persons of the opposite gender.

The ability to procreate impinges powerfully upon adolescence. In our culture, where adolescence includes education and preparation for work that will enable the young adult to be independent of parental support, parenthood in adolescence is premature and is a major impediment. It also precludes development toward completion of the separation-individuation process. The adolescent who becomes a parent is not able to separate from her own parents, and probably is acting on unresolved oedipal factors or even symbiotic wishes to have a baby to cuddle. Often teenage mothers tire of their babies when the child becomes more independent.

The turmoil of adolescence resembles the turmoil of an earlier phase—rapprochement. There the child is in impossible conflict because he wants two incompatible things at once. The adolescent is in a similar position because she wants to be an adult and a dependent child alternately or at the same time.

Marriage as a Developmental Phase

We (Blanck and Blanck 1968) proposed that marriage is a developmental phase appropriate to young adulthood. It follows adolescence and leads to the next developmental phase—parenthood. This is consistent with the theme, first suggested by Erikson (1959) and affirmed by others, that development proceeds throughout life. Most accelerated in the first three years of life, it continues in its differing phases throughout life at a slower pace than at first.

Marriage used to be the first time that a person, especially a woman, left home. Although that does not apply now, marriage, nevertheless, is a permanent separation from the parental family. Added to Blos's idea that another round of the separation-individuation process takes place in adolescence, is that still another round takes place with marriage. This is why marriage is not simply a legal or religious institution. But whether it can truly fulfill its developmental purpose depends once again on whether the first and second rounds of separation-individuation have taken place adequately—the first in the early years, the second in adolescence.

Marriage involves sex in a way different from before. Although sex before marriage is ubiquitous these days, it is different in marriage because the assumption is that there will now be only one sex partner. And more than the sex act is involved here. Much depends on the degree to which oedipal conflicts still dominate. To fulfill the requirements of a developmental phase, sex in marriage represents forgoing one's oedipal objects.

Perhaps in no other relationship is level of object relations more relevant than in marriage. Mahler designated the last subphase of the separation-individuation process as "on-the-way-to-object-constancy." She intended to convey that object constancy is approached but not fully attained at psychological birth, implying that its attainment is a lifelong process. That idea has important implications for later phases of life, perhaps most pronounced in marriage where object constancy plays such a major role. Object constancy does not mean fidelity, although it may influence whether a spouse chooses to be faithful.

We remind ourselves here that object constancy consists of maintenance of a constant mental representation of the object regardless of the state of need (Hartmann). This means that one can be not only in need, but even frustrated and angry without losing the object representation.

Parenthood as a Developmental Phase

This phase has been addressed by Benedek (1959). She proposed that the conflicts of the parents' childhoods are worked over in the experience of parenthood, leading to a new phase in the maturation of the parents. The object representations of the child are established as part of the psychic structure of the parent.

Developmental theory describes how development proceeds throughout life. Remaining to be studied are middle age, young old age, old age, and death. Especially as people are living longer, attention must be paid to how they use their lives. The influence of earlier developmental phases is a determining factor in how old age, infirmity, and even death are approached.

15

What Lies Ahead?

Philosophers and scientists have pondered for centuries about the mind–body problem. Until now the contribution of psychoanalysis has been labored. Freud learned from Charcot that the mind can paralyze the body. But the solution, hypnosis, did not work well and shed no light on how mind and body interact.

In the 1950s psychanalysis entered an overenthusiastic psychosomatic era. Although there is no doubt that mind and body are related and interact, theorists of that time attributed almost every known ailment to psychological causes. Personalities were profiled according to the type of illness. There were ulcer personalities, hypertensive personalities, colitis personalities, and many others. We still believe that even the common cold can be brought about by emotional factors. But by and large, the psychosomatic thinking was too pat. The germ theory of disease was all but abandoned. While there is no doubt that emotions play a role in these and other illnesses, the manner in which the mind influences the body is not so simplistic.

This is not to refute psychosomatics. There remains the question of why some people fall ill and others do not, while germs are everywhere. We speculate that psychological stress lowers the immune system, making physical illness more likely at such times. This still does not provide the answer. Many persons under psychological stress do not become physically ill. The well-known soldier in the trenches under severe stress cannot afford to become ill.

Differentiation of Psyche and Soma

Psyche and soma may be regarded as a unity at the beginning of life. Gradual differentiation takes place, but never totally. It is most likely that the progress of psyche-soma differentiation does not proceed in a straight line. There are moments of relative differentiation, followed by reunion of the two elements, followed by another round of differentiation. The pattern resembles differentiation and integration in psychological development as described by Hartmann. This is not to assert that these two paths proceed in parallel. They might, but we have no way of knowing that.

Psyche and soma never differentiate completely. Perhaps therein lies a clue to the mind–body problem. The solution may be sought in the direction of how they interact. Spitz led psychosomatic theory away from the simplicity of the post–World War II era. He studied the time immediately after birth when the neonate is undifferentiated and reacts in totalities. This can be observed in almost every aspect of infant behavior. Both pleasure and unpleasure produce observable physiological reactions. The smiling child may be seen smiling with her entire body, almost levitating from the crib and smiling down to her feet.

In a most profound excursion into embryology as an analogy, Spitz showed how differentiation and specialization of function occur. There is a turning point in the maturation of an embryo when specialization begins. Then, that which will develop into an eye can no longer serve to develop into an ear, whereas before that point, any part of the embryo was the same as any other. Psychological differentiation may be illustrated in the way that expression of pleasure becomes differentiated and specialized. The older child no longer smiles with her feet. The smile is restricted to the facial muscles. The feet will be used for walking.

One promising pathway to understanding the mind–body problem is investigation of the role of affect. Affective experience predominates in early life, practically to the exclusion of all other modes of perception. Emotions dominate behavior throughout life and have profound reflection in the body—in the musculature, the nervous system, the cardiovascular system, and upon the immune system altogether.

Spitz (1972) attributes psychosomatic disease to the random discharge of primal emotions. In his very attempt to put into words that which is hardly possible to express in the secondary process, Spitz was aware that he could only stumble: "Forgive me if in my attempt at orientation I stumble over my own mixed metaphors when I speak of the bond between affect and percept as a bridge, made of duration, anticipation and meaning; a bridge to span the void across the chasm in front of the soma, a bridge reaching toward the shore of an as yet nonexistent psychic system" (p. 734).

The coenesthetic mode of sensing is fundamental to understanding the mind–body question. This is the mode of reception that exists at the beginning of life when mind and body are one. We never abandon it, although Western civilization plays it down. Some believe that the Eastern religions and practices that, in essence, encourage reversion to the coenesthetic mode bring the individual closer to the unity of mind and body. One reads of the lesser incidence of cardiac problems in the East. Most reports attribute this to diet. Is it only because the Japanese eat more fish? Are the reports leaving something out?

As I have already described, Emde continued Spitz's pursuit of the role of emotion in mental life. He made the remarkable observation that it is affect that provides cohesion and degree of stability in the midst of the turmoil of development.

We are now headed in the direction of a solution by another route—the collaboration between psychoanalysts and neuroscientists who are studying the interface between those two heretofore separate disciplines.

Psychopharmacology

Before returning to that profound collaboration, I have to take a detour through the role of psychopharmacology, the prevailing treatment for psychological problems, especially by psychiatrists. A tendency exists to polarize. Treatment for depression, for example, is thought to be either antidepressants or psychotherapy. The chief of psychiatry at one of our major medical centers declared that he would be doing his residents a disservice if he were to teach them psychotherapy because, he contended, it is no longer needed. The neuroscientists have already proven him wrong. Psychotherapy, they have shown, affects the brain. In some cases, such as depression, medication combined with psychotherapy works best.

When Is Medication Desirable?

Medication is essential in psychosis and in most depressions. Popular opinion, promoted by third-party payers, holds that medication alone suffices. Medication does not substitute for psychotherapy. It can be an adjunct. It can make depressed or withdrawn patients more available for the work that psychotherapy demands of them. I have shown that the capacity to extract from the therapist is a major factor in the success of psychotherapy. Medication can restore that capacity when, for example, it is diminished by depression.

If the therapist is licensed to prescribe, then the matter is all in her hands. The therapist who is not licensed to prescribe medication should, nevertheless, not leave matters entirely in the hands of the psychopharmacologist. Decision about prescriptions should be a collaboration in which the psychotherapist remains in charge of the case. Only the psychotherapist knows when the patient has changed structurally and may no longer need a drug that was prescribed at a different time.

Shortcomings of Psychopharmacology

Medications for the psychoses appear to be more precise than for other disorders. We have a number of drugs for schizophrenia and for the manic-depressive psychosis. For other problems, especially for depression, the drugs that are available are imprecise. I continue to stress that depression is not a diagnostic entity, but a symptom with differing underlying structures. A drug that might be effective for one type of depression may not be so for another.

Often, especially in neurosis, depression and guilt go hand in hand. We do not have medication for guilt. Can this be why medication is not effective in all depressions?

A complicating factor is lack of knowledge about how an individual body will react to a given medication. What is known is that all medications have side effects, some tolerable and some undesirable.

Medication in the Borderline States

This is a condition difficult to diagnose and even more difficult to medicate. Shall the patient be given a drug for psychosis, depression, or both? Decisions have to be made on a case-by-case basis. And, perhaps more than in the other pathologies, the diagnosis is likely to change in the course of appropriate treatment. Although a low-level borderline patient is likely to require antipsychotic medication, a middle-level borderline patient may need to be medicated only until psychotherapy has achieved improvement.

What about Anxiety?

We now have many anti-anxiety drugs. To prescribe them responsibly, again a differential diagnosis according to structure is in order. Anti-anxiety drugs as well as antidepressants are sometimes helpful to enable the patient to function and to engage in psychotherapy. Severe anxiety is to be alleviated until psychotherapy takes effect.

To be borne in mind is that mild and temporary anxiety is the affect that results from neurotic conflict. It is always desirable to work on the conflict rather than obscure it. That is an old tenet in the practice of medicine—do not prescribe medication that obscures symptoms if the patient can tolerate the discomfort for the sake of a more lasting cure.

Obsessive-Compulsive Disorders

Some obsessive-compulsive patients need medication. I have already discussed that this is not a single disorder. Medication is indicated for those who are presumed to have a chemical imbalance in the brain. We are on shaky ground here.

What Position to Take?

The drugs now available help many people but do not help every-one. Buried behind the enthusiasm for those depressions that are helped lie severe depressions that do not respond to anything known today. Precisely how do these drugs affect the brain? It is acknowledged that they do not zero in on the particular part of the brain where they might be most effective. They may be compared with buckshot; sometimes they hit their target. A new category of drugs is being developed that promises greater pre-cision; they will affect that part of the brain that produces the chemical part of the larger problem.

Limitations

Drugs cannot alter structure nor build object relations. It has been established that there are organic factors in most psychoses. Very likely, those prevent the neonate and young child from entering into the affective object relationship that will build structure. When we provide medication for an adult patient, or perhaps even for a child, we know that drugs can alter mood and behavior. They cannot substitute for growth-promoting life experience.

Where Are We Now?

I have implied that brain chemistry is only one part of a larger matter. There are other factors:

1. The anatomy of the individual brain: Just as the more observable aspects of the human body vary, so it must be with brains. We can be fairly certain that not all brains are the same.

2. The neuronal firings: If the brain could be observed in action, what would we see? How do chemical and electrical factors interact?
3. Hormonal effect: Is this part of the chemistry, or a separate but related factor?
4. The structures that have been laid down: I have described the likelihood that experience alters the physical structure of the brain. This is certainly an individual matter, for establishment of structure is dependent on the life experience.

Neuropsychology

Neuropsychology is a burgeoning discipline that is making new discoveries almost daily. Ultimately, neurology, chemistry, and psychotherapy will have to be coordinated to learn how these act upon the brain and other parts of the nervous system. The situation is not static. A new and more promising class of drugs is being developed; our knowledge and skill in psychotherapy is advancing; study of the human brain is facilitated by development of new instrumentation.

Where Do the Answers Lie?

It has been shown that affects can effect structural changes in the brain. That is why psychotherapy is effective and why it is more lasting than medication. Medication does its work only when it is used. Psychotherapy creates permanent alteration.

Progress in understanding the workings of the brain is proceeding apace. The complete answer is not yet within our grasp. Human interaction will continue to be the major factor because of considerations of structure, internalization, and object relations. Drugs cannot provide the affective experience in self and object relations that makes us human.

The Future

The future of psychoanalytic developmental psychology is intricately bound up with future discoveries in psychopharmacology and in the neurosciences. When it all comes together, we will have more precise medications that will zero in on the exact area of the brain that needs alteration. We will also know more about the effect on the brain of affective experience in life and in psychotherapy.

The new science, then, will be a unified one that takes all factors into account. It will consist of the merger of neuroscience, psychopharmacology, and psychology. Psychoanalytic developmental theory already plays an important role in contributing toward this unification.

Annotated Bibliography

American Psychiatric Association (1994). *Diagnostic and Statistical Manual of Mental Disorders, 4th ed. (DSM-IV)*. Washington, DC: APA.

This is the standard manual that presents diagnosis and diagnostic codes uniformly. It has value for administrative and statistical purposes. It does not provide a guide to treatment because it is atheoretical and because it diagnoses by symptom rather than by structure.

Benedek, T. (1959). Parenthood as a developmental phase. *Journal of the American Psychoanalytic Association* 7:389–417.

Benedek pioneered developmental theory when it was barely becoming part of psychoanalytic thinking. She appreciated that development does not cease in early life, but continues into adulthood. She chose to consider parenthood in developmental terms. Her theoretical position came about when theory construction was beginning to make the transition from drive theory only to drive theory enhanced by ego psychology. Her vocabulary is much in the language of drive theory because that is more familiar to her. The result is that she introduces profound developmental factors that she must express somewhat awkwardly in drive theory language. Nevertheless, this paper is a major contribution to developmental theory, especially as it shows how both parents find developmental opportunity in interaction with their child.

Blanck, G. (1966). Some technical implications of ego psychology. *International Journal of Psycho-Analysis* 47:389–417.

This paper proposes that ego psychological concepts influence and expand the technical repertory. Emphasis is upon the repetition in the analytic situation of developmental issues that offer opportunity for reworking. It suggests that the treatment be "tailored" to provide for ego growth. The separation process is especially emphasized as a feature of development, and it is suggested that it be used technically.

———— (1984). The complete Oedipus complex. *International Journal of Psycho-Analysis* 65:331–339.

The Oedipus complex is reconsidered here in its positive and negative forms, completely, as Freud described. The sexual and hostile features apply to both parents at different times. Added is the object relations feature. It is suggested that, instead of a triangle, we use a straight-line diagram to depict the oedipal child moving back and forth while a parent representation remains fixed at either pole. The distance from one parent representation or the other shows the nature of the child's object relatedness at a given time.

———— (1987). *How to Be a Good Enough Parent: The Subtle Seductions.* Northvale, NJ: Jason Aronson.

This book is addressed to parents to show them how developmental features in their child may be exploited for the child's maximum development. It describes the life stories of five adults to show how pathology might have been averted had the parents intervened appropriately at the age-specific developmental time.

Blanck, G., and Blanck, R. (1972). Toward a psychoanalytic developmental psychology. *Journal of the American Psychoanalytic Association* 20:668–710.

Twelve books on development are considered in an essay that integrates those that are consistent one with the other. It was determined that the works of Spitz and Mahler stand out as complementary and as contributing toward a unified psychoanalytic developmental psychology.

———— (1974). *Ego Psychology: Theory and Practice*, 2nd ed. New York: Columbia University Press, 1994.

This is a textbook of ego psychology. It summarizes the contributions of the major ego psychologists and shows how these concepts may be used clinically to treat narcissistic and borderline patients as well as neurotics.

———— (1979). *Ego Psychology II: Psychoanalytic Development Psychology.* New York: Columbia University Press.

Psychoanalytic development theory matures as the authors show its relevance in diagnosis, in psychoanalytic treatment, and in the treatment of the borderline and narcissistic personalities.

———— (1980). Separation-individuation: an organizing principle. In *Rapprochement: The Critical Subphase of Separation-Individuation*, ed. R. F. Lax, S. Bach, and J. A. Burland, pp. 101–116. New York: Jason Aronson.

This paper proposes that the separation-individuation process serves ego organization.

———— (1988). The contribution of ego psychology in understanding the process of termination in psychoanalysis and psychotherapy. *Journal of the American Psychoanalytic Association* 36:961–984.

This paper shows the value of the separation-individuation process in termination and how unfinished separation issues may be furthered in the process of separating from the analyst at termination.

Blanck, R. (1986). The function of the object representations. *Psychotherapie, Psychosomatics and Mediscine Psychologie* 36:1–7. Stuttgart: Thieme.

Here it is proposed that the functions of the object representations are taken over by the self representations in the course of development. Internalization becomes a three-step process whereby selected functions are first copied, then internalized, and finally relegated to the self representations. Each step in the process leads to greater degree of independence.

Blanck, R., and Blanck, G. (1968). *Marriage and Personal Development*. New York: Columbia University Press.

Marriage is seen as a developmental phase in which the young adult acquires a greater degree of separation, abandons incestuous wishes by seeking a nonincestuous partner, and takes yet another step in the waning of oedipal wishes.

——— (1977). The transference object and the real object. *International Journal of Psycho-Analysis* 58:33–44.

This paper pursues the observations made by Greenson and Zetzel that the analyst is perceived, not only as an object from the past in the transference, but as a real person in the present as well. It stresses the representations of the object rather than the object in reality.

——— (1986). *Beyond Ego Psychology: Developmental Object Relations Theory.* New York: Columbia University Press.

The book continues the ego psychology series, this time pursuing the object relations factor in the treatment situation. Also proposed is a revision of structural theory to assert that the ego is a superordinate agency that exercises the function of organizing the psychic apparatus.

Blos, P. (1962). *On Adolescence: A Psychoanalytic Interpretation.* New York: Free Press.

The separation-individuation process proceeds through a second round in adolescence as the child-not-yet-adult struggles for independence within remaining still dependent.

Edgecombe, R., and Burgner, M. (1975). The phallic-narcissistic phase differentiation between preoedipal and oedipal aspects of phallic development. *Psychoanalytic Study of the Child* 30:161–180. New Haven, CT: Yale University Press.

The authors discuss the difference between preoedipal and oedipal investment in the body. They question whether there can be a phallic phase in girls.

Emde, R. N. (1988a). Development terminable and interminable, part 1: innate and emotional factors from infancy. *International Journal of Psycho-Analysis* 69:23–42.

Following Harmann and Spitz, the author proposes that development is based on the interaction of the endowment with the environment, and that development continues throughout life.

———— (1988b). Development terminable and interminable, part 2: recent psychoanalytic theory and therapeutic considerations. *International Journal of Psycho-Analysis* 69:283–296.

This continues from part 1 and stresses therapeutic consequences of this expanded theory.

———— (1999). Moving ahead: integrating influences of affective processes for development and for psychoanalysis. *International Journal of Psycho-Analysis* 79:80–317.

Here it is proposed that affect is an essential feature of the developmental process. It serves to maintain cohesion of the psychic system in the midst of developmental change.

Erikson, E. H. (1959). *Identity and the Life Cycle. Psychological Issues. Monograph 1*. New York: International Universities Press.

This book is one of the first to recognize that development proceeds throughout life. The life cycle is traced and described in terms sometimes coinciding with and sometimes at variance with the ego psychological studies. Some of the ego psychologists regard Erikson's work as more sociological, whereas the ego psychological bent is more toward internal processes.

Federn, P. (1952). *Ego Psychology and the Psychoses*. New York: Basic Books.

Federn was one of the "spin-off" theorists whose work flowed directly from Freud's proposal of the structural theory. While Hartmann studied the ego in normal development, Federn examined the psychotic ego.

Fenichel, O. (1931). *Problems of Psychoanalytic Technique*. New York: Psychoanalytic Quarterly.

This is a classic. It is the standard text of psychoanalytic technique. Since it precedes ego psychology, much has been added to the theory of technique. Nevertheless, this work remains basic to the literature on technique.

Freud, A. (1936). The ego and the mechanisms of defense. In *The Writings of Anna Freud*, vol. 2. New York: International Universities Press.

This is Anna Freud's landmark work on the defensive function of the ego. She enumerates the major defense mechanisms, shows how they function in defending against anxiety. Included is an introductory chapter on technique.

Freud, S. (1900). The interpretation of dreams. *Standard Edition* 4/5: 1–626.

> Many believe that, had Freud contributed only this work, it would have earned a place in the history of psychoanalysis. Here Freud proposes his dream theory and shows how dreams are constructed. He uses his own dreams as examples. He provided a theory that explains the primary process and symbolism. In recent times his dream theory has been validated by independent study. It remains viable and is used in psychoanalytic treatment as an indispensable tool. Freud regarded dreams as the "royal road" to the unconscious. Dreams are not used in that way invariably now. Since the adaptive and defensive structures and the object relations factor have come into the psychoanalytic picture, dreams are also used to deal with those matters, and as a way of propelling the treatment.

——— (1905). Three essays on the theory of sexuality. *Standard Edition* 7:121–145.

> Freud discovered in his clinical work that there is childhood sexuality and he took the bold step of announcing it to the scientific community, which became alarmed. It might be regarded as the first child observational study even though Freud did not observe children, but gathered his data from adult patients in treatment with him. Without it there could hardly be a theory of psychoanalysis, and certainly developmental theory could not have come about.

——— (1909a). Analysis of a phobia in five-year-old boy. *Standard Edition* 10:3–149.

This is one for Freud's five case histories. It recounts the analysis of "Little Hans," a boy whose father conducted the analysis of the child under Freud's tutelage. It is the first recorded child analysis. Although flawed in many ways by today's standards, especially because it was the father who conducted the analysis, it nevertheless led the way to development of child analysis as a specialty of analysis proper.

——— (1909b). Notes upon a case of obsessional neurosis. *Standard Edition* 10:153–318.

This is another of Freud's case histories. It is known by its nickname of the Rat Man. Here Freud traces the convoluted thinking of an obsession. Thrown into question these days is whether the patient was truly neurotic, or rather borderline. That diagnostic distinction was not yet made. Freud thought he was presenting a case of neurosis. Despite the contemporary questions, we learn much about the workings of the obsessional mind.

——— (1911). Psychoanalytic notes on a case of paranoia. *Standard Edition* 12:3–82.

Here Freud records his study of the memoirs of a paranoid schizophrenic, written while the author was confined to a mental institution. Out of this study, Freud learned about the operation of projection in paranoia and about the homosexual element.

——— (1912). The dynamics of the transference. *Standard Edition* 12:97–108.

Here Freud raises the question of why transference is so powerful and answers it by explaining that it represents regression to early object love. He also discusses transference as resistance, a matter that makes the treatment difficult for the analyst. However, he notes, transference makes the patient's forgotten love emotions manifest.

——— (1914). On narcissism: an introduction. *Standard Edition* 14:67–102.

In this paper, Freud begins his study of what we may now designate as self and object relations theory. He examines both normal and pathological narcissism and describes object choice. The narcissistic type loves himself, what he once was, what he would like to be, and someone who was once part of himself. It is worthy of note that the latter anticipates Mahler by some sixty years. Mahler's finding that the infant and developing child experiences herself as in some degree part of the object representations is a cornerstone of her theory.

The anaclitic type loves the woman who tends and the man who protects. Today this would be recognized as normal narcissism, or better still, normal self and object relations.

——— (1917). Mourning and melancholia. *Standard Edition* 14:237–258.

In this paper, Freud distinguishes between normal mourning and depression. In mourning the world seems cold and empty. In depression, the self feels cold and empty.

——— (1918). From the history of an infantile neurosis. *Standard Edition* 17:3–123.

This is one of Freud's five case histories, nicknamed the Wolf Man. Again it has been questioned whether this patient was truly neurotic, or rather borderline. But at that time Freud's interest lay not only in treatment, but also in discovery of theory through his case material. This case conveys the idea that the child is frightened by the primal scene. Freud discovered this through a dream in which the patient saw wolves on the limbs of a tree. Freud traced this to a forgotten memory of exposure to the primal scene.

——— (1923). The ego and the id. *Standard Edition* 19:12–68.

This paper enunciates the structural theory and marks a major shift in theory construction. It resulted from Freud's discovery, in his clinical work, that part of the ego is unconscious. Now structure is tripartite, with the addition of the superego as a differential grade within the ego. This work became the point of departure for the evolution of ego psychology.

——— (1937). Analysis terminable and interminable. *Standard Edition* 23:209–253.

Here Freud discusses the limits of the analytic endeavor. The material that can be analyzed derives from the past as it influences the present. We cannot analyze that which is yet to come. Sometimes an analysis provides the ability to deal competently with later events. Sometimes later events create a situation calling for further analysis.

Freud, S., and Breuer, J. (1893–1895). Studies in hysteria. *Standard Edition* 2:196–201.

> Upon his return from Charcot's clinic in Paris where he learned hypnosis, Freud attempted to collaborate with Josef Breuer, a senior neurologist, in the treatment of a case of hysteria. Breuer gave up the case when the patient, a young woman, expressed erotic feelings toward him. Freud recognized this as a transference phenomenon. This was the beginning of our understanding of the issue of the transference as the prime event in psychoanalytic treatment.

Galenson, E., and Roiphe, H. (1976). Some suggested revisions concerning early female development. *Journal of the American Psychoanalytic Association* 24:29–57.

> These findings represent child observational studies in a nursery school setting. It was observed that very young girls experience a form of castration shock upon noticing the anatomical difference between girls and boys.

Greenacre, P. (1959). Certain technical problems in the transference relationship. *Journal of the American Psychoanalytic Association* 7:484–502.

> Greenacre recognizes the special position of the transference in psychoanalytic therapy and elaborates on the problems that these create and their technical solutions.

——— (1972). Problems of overidealization of the analyst and of analysis: their manifestation in the transference and countertransference relationship. *Psychoanalytic Study of the Child* 20:209–219. New York: International Universities Press.

Greenacre looks at the young child's fascination with the father as experiences with him are registered affectively and reactivated in the transference. This provides us with important insight into the development of the child and the role of the father in that development. His first task is to lure the child out of the symbiotic relationship with the mother so that the child can enter the long separation-individuation process. As the father becomes more distinct from the mother because object experience gradually replaces need and self-interest, the father is seen as another person, different from the mother. In the days when most mothers were at home while the father went to work, his homecoming in the evening became an important developmental opportunity for the child. The father brought an aura of a mysterious outside world and the child became entranced with it and with him. Greenacre notes how this reappears in the transference and warns that the analyst be aware of this in the countertransference lest idealization of the situation be repeated without therapeutic benefit.

Greenson, R. R. (1964). The working alliance and the transference neurosis. *Psychoanalytic Quarterly* 34:155–181.

Greenson proposes that the relationship with the analyst does not consist of the transference neurosis only. There is a part of the relationship that is real and consists of the patient's joining the analyst in the realistic purpose of curing the neurosis. He termed this feature of the analytic relationship "the working alliance."

——— (1967). *The Technique and Practice of Psychoanalysis.* New York: Hallmark.

This is the first of a proposed two-volume work that attempts to bring technique up to date. Unfortunately, Greenson died before he could write the second volume. Copiously illustrated with clinical material, Greenson illuminates the method of psychoanalysis and the techniques he pursues.

Hartmann, H. (1958). *Ego Psychology and the Problem of Adaptation.* New York: International Universities Press.

This is Hartmann's major work, which spins off from Freud's enunciation of the structural theory. Hartmann concerned himself with psychoanalysis as a normal psychology as well as a psychopathology. By focusing on the adaptive function of the ego, Hartmann became the father of ego psychology.

Hartmann defined adaptation as the reciprocal relationship between the organism and its environment, thus paving the way for study of the interaction between mother and infant in the process of the infant's development.

Benedeck found that this is not a one-way street—that the parent develops in her and his own way in concert with the child's development.

Hartmann developed the concept of the undifferentiated matrix out of which ego and id arise; the conflict-free sphere of the ego that functions outside of the arena of conflict. He regarded it as normal that creative thinking takes a detour through fantasy. He dealt with object relations and with how structuralization serves adaptation. He considered object relations, intelligence, rationality, and thinking.

Hartmann, H., and Kris, E. (1945). The genetic approach in psychoanalysis. *Psychoanalytic Study of the Child* 1:11–30. New York: International Universities Press.

Here the authors deal with the factors of metapsychology. To the established ones of the structural, dynamic, and economic, they add the genetic. The genetic approach explains why early experience exerts influence on later life.

Hartmann, H., and Loewenstein, R. M. (1946). Comments on the formation of psychic structure. *Psychoanalytic Study of the Child* 2:11–30. New York: International Universities Press.

This is the place where the authors weave together drive theory and ego psychology. They also emphasize the concepts of differentiation and integration. "Differentiation indicates the specialization of a function; integration the emergence of a new function" (p. 18). It is by differentiation that the ego becomes a specialized organ, separate from the id. This distinguishes the instinctual drives of humans from the instincts of animals. Animals rely on their instinct to adjust to reality; humans mediate through the ego, an organ separate from the id.

——— (1949). Notes on the theory of aggression. *Psychoanalytic Study of the Child* 3/4:9–36. New York: International Universities Press.

The authors are puzzled by the fact that libido has a biological avenue of discharge in orgasm, while aggression appears to have none. They neither agree with the theory of a death instinct nor that aggression seeks to destroy. In their attempt to find a theory of aggression, they place emphasis on the need to preserve the object. This is accomplished by displacement, restricting the aim of the drive, sublimation, and fusion of aggression with libido in which libido dominates.

————— (1962). Notes on the superego. *Psychoanalytic Study of the Child* 17:42–81. New York: International Universities Press.

The authors agree with Freud that the superego is the structure that crystallizes out of the oedipal conflict. The beginning internalizations are the ingredients that ultimately cohere to form the superego.

Jacobson, E. (1964). *The Self and the Object World.* New York: International Universities Press.

Having written a paper with the same title, Jacobson now expands what is essentially the object relations theory of ego psychology. She makes the transition from psychoanalysis as a drive theory only to psychoanalysis as a drive, ego psychological, object relations, and conflict theory. This makes the reading difficult because she has to struggle with the language of drive theory, not yet able to express herself in the new language of ego psychology. Thus we are obliged to translate ego psychological concepts from drive theory language. Her contribution is so outstanding that it is worth the effort.

Jacobson deals with identity formation and with the distinction between ego, self, and self representation. She carries forward Hartmann's concept of a representational world, a cornerstone of ego psychological object relations theory. Self representation and object representations arise out of experience of the self in interaction with the object. This connotes that there is an internal representational world, not the same as the external world, but influenced by experience. Jacobson did extensive work on depression and on depersonalization as a normal phenomenon in unusually stressful situations.

Kandel, E. (1990). Paper presented at the plenary session of the American Psychoanalytic Association.

With slides, Kandel illustrated his experiment with worms to show that structure is built with repeated stimuli. He applied an electric current to the organism and, upon dissection, found that a physical structure had been laid down. We extrapolate from that that physical structures can be established in the human brain.

Kaplan, L. (1987). Discussion of Daniel Stern's *The Interpersonal World of the Infant. Contemporary Psychoanalysis* 2(1):27.

Kaplan refutes Stern by questioning his methodology. He observed infants at their most alert moments in the laboratory in his attempt to prove that there is a self at birth. Kaplan asserts that there is a difference between the baby at home and that same baby in the laboratory. The "home" baby is more likely to be merged with the mother, as Mahler noted, while the laboratory baby is more alert and can erroneously be believed to be demonstrating the existence of a separate self.

Kernberg, O. (1967). Borderline personality organization. *Journal of the American Psychoanalytic Association* 15:641–685.

Here begins Kernberg's introduction of a theory of the borderline conditions that is destined to become a prominent view of the diagnosis and treatment of that pathology. He regards the borderline patient as having organized a defensive structure different from that of the neurotic. The borderline patient organizes defense against hostility by splitting the representations of the object into all good and all bad. The therapeutic objective is to heal the split.

——— (1976). *Object Relations Theory and Clinical Psychoanalysis*. New York: Jason Aronson.

The etiology of the more severe pathologies lies in the abnormal development of internalized object relations. The drives are first expressed as affects—inborn behavior patterns activated in interaction with the maternal object. This leads to internalization of object relations and to affective memory.

Knight, R. P. (1954). Borderline States. *Psychoanalytic Psychiatry and Psychology*, ed. R. R. Knight and C. Friedman, pp. 52–64. New York: International Universities Press.

Knight pioneered in studying the borderline conditions at a time when they were not at all understood. Analysts followed Freud's method of trial analysis. However, many patients continued long beyond Freud's two-week trial period before being declared unanalyzable. Taken in historical perspective, Knight pointed the way toward viewing the borderline conditions as a distinct diagnostic category, paving the way for Kernberg to investigate the borderline conditions more thoroughly, for Stone to propose that the scope of psychoanalysis may be expanded to encompass some patients who engage in neurotic conflict but also present some borderline features, and for Mahler to suggest that borderline phenomena represent the failure of completion of the separation-individuation process.

Kohut, H. (1971). *The Analysis of the Self*. New York: International Universities Press.

Kohut presents his theory of narcissism. He asserts that his is the only direct continuation of Freud's work. He omits the contributions of the ego psychologists, who were his contemporaries and whose work was prominent in the literature of the time. He presents a theory of narcissism and shows that, developmentally, it can proceed in normal or deviant directions. These "forms and transformations" of narcissism are seen through observation in the transference.

——— (1977). *The Restoration of the Self*. New York: International Universities Press.

Here is the inception of self psychology. In his earlier work, Kohut dealt principally with pathological narcissism as reflected in the transference. Now he expands his theory to include normal development and to launch a theory of the self. At this juncture in the evolution of theory, self psychology and ego psychology take different paths.

Kris, E. (1951). Ego psychology and interpretation in psychoanalytic therapy. *Psychoanalytic Quarterly* 20:15–30.

Ego psychology, Kris asserts, enlarges the scope of psychoanalysis by applying knowledge of preoedipal life to the analysis of neurotic conflict. He also emphasizes that which Anna Freud had already noted—that resistance used to be regarded as an obstacle when the objective of psychoanalysis was to arrive at the unconscious quickly, but is now looked upon as essential to the defensive process. He defines evenly suspended attention as oscillation among empathy, self-observation, and judgment. And he recommends that interpretation be designed to carry the broadest possible meaning rather than the narrow one of id content only.

——— (1952). *Psychoanalytic Explorations in Art*. New York: International Universities Press.

This is the work in which the capacity to regress in the service of the ego is described. That capacity is used by the artist to regress to the primary process where the raw material for artistic creation is found. The artist recovers from that regression in the "service of the ego" to emerge with a communicable product that is no longer primary process but represents something that may be communicated to an audience. Similarly, the analytic patient regresses in order to be in touch with the primary process and then to bring those matters that reside there into the secondary process—that is, to be able to communicate to the analyst. This book describes how artist, analysand, and others use regression creatively by recovering from it.

——— (1956a). The recovery of childhood memories in psychoanalysis. *Psychoanalytic Study of the Child* 11:54–88. New York: International Universities Press.

Kris shows that childhood memories are the result of telescoping of events that are reprocessed in the course of development so that a single event becomes condensed with later ones and is processed by the later-developed capacitates of the child to become a memory, no longer of a single event, but of many.

——— (1956b). Some vicissitudes of insight in psychoanalysis. *International Journal of Psycho-Analysis* 37:445–455.

This paper is so famous that it acquired a nickname—The Good Hour. It introduces the idea, formerly unknown in psychoanalysis, that intrasystemic conflict is as important as intersystemic conflict. It is the integrative function of the ego that includes both these factors and takes us away from regarding resistance and defense as the sole factors.

The Good Hour begins unpropitiously, even with a negative tinge. This follow Spitz's concept of "No" as a separating device. The patient is seen, as might the developing child who says "I will do it myself." Then there might be a dream, to which the patient associates spontaneously and provides a self-interpretation. Analysis is approaching termination when this happens.

Loewald, H. W. (1980). *Papers on Psychoanalysis.* New Haven, CT: Yale University Press.

This is a collection of Loewald's papers. Some of the outstanding ones are on the therapeutic action of psychoanalysis, in which he details how the analytic process makes for therapeutic change, and his paper on the Oedipus complex, in which he deals with parricidal wishes and their diminution by means of "waning" of the oedipal conflict.

Mahler, M. A. (1971). A study of the separation-individuation process and its possible application to borderline phenomena in the psychoanalytic situation. *Psychoanalytic Study of the Child* 26:403–424. New York: Quadrangle.

Here Mahler considers the vicissitudes of the separation-individuation process to conclude that the borderline conditions are the consequence of incompletion of that process. The individual, not having attained psychological birth, experiences her self representations as in some degree part of the object representations. That each individual experiences a different degree of separateness is what makes diagnosis and treatment of the borderline conditions so difficult to diagnose.

Mahler, M. S., Pine, F., and Bergman, A. (1975). *The Psychological Birth of the Human Infant.* New York: Basic Books.

In this landmark work on developmental theory, the authors summarize their observations of mother–child pairs at the Masters Children's Center in New York. Mahler had already done considerable work on separation-individuation. However, this carefully designed observational study crystallized her hypotheses into a distinct theory by which she was able to assert that psychological birth takes place three years after physical birth through the phases of fitting together, symbiosis, and the long separation-individuation process.

Osofsky, J. D., ed. (1979). *Handbook of Infant Development.* New York: Wiley.

Following upon Spitz's presentation of his concept of ego organization, Osofsky elaborates on infant development along the lines that Spitz suggested.

Rangell, L. (1986). The executive functions of the ego: an extension of the concept of ego autonomy. *Psychoanalytic Study of the Child* 41:1–37. New Haven, CT: Yale University Press.

Rangell expands the list of functions of the ego by attributing to the ego an overall function that is superordinate to the other ego functions. That is an executive function that oversees the cohesion of the entire ego organization.

Sandler, J., and Rosenblatt, B. (1952). The concept of a representational world. *Psychoanalytic Study of the Child* 17: 128–145. New York: International Universities Press.

The authors elaborate on Freud's, Hartmann's and Jacobson's construct of internalization and of the existence of an internal world. They show that there is a "locus" within the ego where internalized representations reside.

Spitz, R. A. (1945). Hospitalism: an inquiry into the genesis of psychiatric conditions in early childhood. *Psychoanalytic Study of the Child* 1:52–74. New York: International Universities Press.

Infants, hospitalized because they were motherless, were suffering from maramus (failure to thrive) and some were dying, despite good nourishment. Spitz was called in to investigate what appeared to be a baffling situation. He found that, indeed, the nourishment was proper but administered in assemblyline fashion, the nurse going from crib to crib and propping the nursing bottles. He concluded that the life-giving ingredient that was lacking was human touch. From this study we have come to appreciate that infants need not only food, but maternal holding and touching.

———— (1959). *A Genetic Field Theory of Ego Formation*. New York: International Universities Press.

Spitz develops his theory of ego formation. There are three stages in this process, each announcing its attainment by an indicator. The first indicator, the smiling response, occurs after a few weeks and indicates that the experiences of the first weeks of life have become organized. The second indicator, stranger anxiety, shows that the child has acquired a "libidinal object proper" and is wary of strangers. This marks an important achievement in the development of object relations. The third indicator, semantic communication, is more than merely acquisition of speech. It connotes that both separation and level of object relations have developed to the point where the child must communicate "across a chasm," the chasm of separation.

———— (1965). *The First Year of Life*. New York: International Universities Press.

Here Spitz reiterates his "field theory," focusing on development within the first year.

———— (1972). Bridges: on anticipation, duration and meaning. *Journal of the American Psychoanalytic Association* 20:721–735.

Here Spitz refers to memory of early experience. By approximately 18 months of age the child will have accumulated so much experience that life itself is unique for each child. These "memories" are not of separate events. They are mute, invisible tides, far more complex than was previously thought, and they exert profound influence on attitudes and behavior in later life.

Stern, D. (1985). *The Interpersonal World of the Infant.* New York: Basic Books.

Stern's work follows after Mahler's and refutes her. He appears to be presenting a developmental theory for self psychology because data from child observation were lacking. Stern proposed to provide it. His methodology, however, is subject to much question because he observed babies in the laboratory, where they were most alert. At other times of the day, and in interaction with their mothers, they are more likely to experience themselves as merged with their mothers. That was what Mahler discovered as she observed, not infants, but mother–infant pairs. To provide a theory for self psychology, Stern asserts that there is a self at birth, while Mahler found that it takes approximately three years from physical to psychological birth—for the acquisition of a self representation separate from the object representations. From a scientific point of view, one must question whether a priori derived conclusions that are sought for a particular purpose may be regarded as valid.

Stone, L. (1954). The widening scope of indications for psychoanalysis. *Journal of the American Psychoanalytic Association* 2:567–594.

At this early time in the discovery of diagnosis and treatment of the less-than-neurotic patient, Stone discovered that there are such patients who are nevertheless treatable by the analytic method if one tailors the treatment to their special needs. This, he proposed, widened the scope of analy-

zability for many patients. If we adhere to Kernberg's designation of high level borderline, perhaps these patients
would coincide diagnostically with those that Stone includes within the realm of analyzability. There are many
patients who are sufficiently structured to be able to endure
conflict, and yet who manifest some borderline features.
Stone brings them into the realm of analyzability.

Index

About the Author

Gertrude Blanck holds a B.A. from Hunter College, an M.S. from Columbia University, and a Ph.D. from New York University. She has had extensive psychoanalytical training and has been in the private practice of psychoanalysis and psychotherapy since 1950. At a time when little was known about the technique of psychotherapy, Dr. Blanck established the Institute for the Study of Psychotherapy where she, along with a distinguished faculty, trained hundreds of psychotherapists who are now themselves teachers. An esteemed supervisor and seminar leader, she has lectured in the major cities of the United States, Europe, China, and the Philippines. She is coauthor of the noted trilogy *Ego Psychology: Theory and Practice, Ego Psychology II: Psychoanalytic Developmental Psychology*, and *Beyond Ego Psychology*; and the author of *How to Be a Good-Enough Parent*, as well as several papers in the psychoanalytic journals. A member of the American Psychological Association and an honorary member of the North Carolina Psychoanalytic Society, Dr. Blanck is past president of the Institute for Psychoanalytic Training and Research, Distinguished Lydia Rapaport Visiting Professor at Smith College, and recipient of the Margaret S. Mahler Memorial Award. She has been named to the Hunter College Hall of Fame.